Praise ʃ
Miracle

MW01115157

"Life is a journey that is to be explored. This incredible offering from Jennifer Colt brings forth some of the most illuminating lessons that can often only be learned in the darkest of times.

Colt offers up her own path as evidence that living in two worlds—the physical and the metaphysical—with one spirit is not only possible but practical. *Minor Mercies & Big Ass-Miracles* is a bold case for the gap that closes between Heaven and Earth...always on time and in perfect order...if we simply listen and follow."

—John St. Augustine, Gracie Award-winning Radio Host and Author of Every Moment Matters

Praise for the McAfee Twins Novels
By Jennifer Colt

"I got a real kick out of the story, and only hope there will soon be another madcap crime spree in Hollywood for the McAfee Twins to solve."

—Elizabeth Gilbert, author of *Eat, Pray, Love*

"Fast and furious, and the laughs keep coming."

—Barnes and Noble Editors

"A fast-paced, gum-snapping, snarky chick-lit mystery with sparkle to spare."

—Publishers Weekly

"Wild, entertaining."

—Booklist

"Jennifer Colt impales readers upon her rapier-sharp wit, and then proceeds to make them laugh until they cry."

—Curled Up with a Good Book

"A ripping great read."

—Midwest Book Review

Also by Jennifer Colt

The McAfee Twins Novels

The Butcher of Beverly Hills: A Novel (2005)

The Mangler of Malibu Canyon: A Novel (2006)

The Vampire of Venice Beach: A Novel (2007)

The Con Artist of Catalina Island: A McAfee Twins Christmas Novel (2007)

The Hellraiser of the Hollywood Hills: A McAfee Twins Novel (2010)

Minor Mercies &

BIG-ASS MIRACLES

A Writer's Spiritual Journey that Stops
Just Short of Nirvana

Jennifer Colt

Santa Monica, California

Published by Tessera Books

Published in the United States by Tessera Books, a division of
Tessera Productions, Inc., Santa Monica, California.

Library of Congress-in Publication Data

Colt, Jennifer

Minor mercies & big-ass miracles: how i became a screenwriter
and author using the science of mind /

Jennifer Colt. — 2nd ed.

p. cm.

1. Colt, Jennifer—Writing. 2. Self-Help. 3. Spirituality—
Metaphysics. 4. Religion—Religious Science. 1, Title.

With self-deprecating humor, Jennifer Colt chronicles her path to
publication through prayer and the application of spiritual
principles such as the Law of Attraction.

ISBN - 13: 978-1460926826
ISBN - 10: 146092682X

LCCN   2011922993
10 9 8 7 6 5 4 3 2

Dedication

*T*his book is dedicated to Dr. David Walker. I can hear you belting out show tunes from the other side.

Acknowledgments

*T*hank God for talented and tolerant friends.

I could not have managed this departure from my usual fare without the help and support of one Brett Ellen Block. What a gal, what a pal.

Barbara Davilman and Tom Meshelski, thank you for your invaluable feedback.

Thanks also to everyone who let me use their proper names, and to those whose names I withheld while nevertheless embarrassing them.

And a special appreciation for Claudia, who is a miracle unto herself.

Minor Mercies &

BIG-ASS MIRACLES

"*T*he truth will set you free, but first it will really piss you off."

—Dr. David Walker, former minister of the Los
Angeles Center for Spiritual Living

"*I* believe. Help thou my unbelief."

—Conflicted Bible Person

Introduction

*I*f you're one of those people who got all excited about *The Secret* a few years ago, only to be disappointed when a super hot genie with a British accent didn't arrive on your doorstep to grant all of your wishes the very next day, this book is for you.

It's also for those who people attended my readings and asked, "How did you find your agent?" and "How did you get published?" but didn't receive an honest answer because I was too chicken to admit in public: I prayed for it.

The truth is, I've been using the Law of Attraction and the other principles laid out in Ernest Holmes's book *The Science of Mind* for fourteen years, and the theme—nay, the whole point of this book—is that this stuff *really, really works.*

When I began my spiritual journey in the late 90's, I was broke, separated, depressed, and very far from the goal I'd moved from Texas to Los Angeles to accomplish, that of becoming a professional writer. On the recommendation of a friend I attended a metaphysical church housed in an Art Deco movie theater on Wilshire Boulevard, two doors down from Larry Flynt Publications. (Only in LA.) The preacher was a large, hilarious man who regularly broke out into soft shoe routines or songs from Broadway musicals during his talks.

In this unlikeliest of places I found my salvation.

Once I began the study of metaphysics things turned around in a way that was nothing short of miraculous. I reconciled with my husband, found a great place to live, got work as a screenwriter for Miramax—this, as a woman over forty in a business dominated by young men, with no agent and no credits—and wound up with a publishing deal at Random House.

In retrospect it looks easy, but at the time I was racked with self-doubt. My biggest fear was that the men in the white coats would break into the house and drag me, kicking and screaming about consciousness, straight to the booby hatch. When you begin to embrace these ideas there will be times when you think you've slipped your moorings and become a mouth–foaming, delusional lunatic.

My advice? *Feel the crazy and do it anyway.* Altering your worldview is essential to changing your life. Everything is set in motion through your willingness to suspend disbelief.

God knows I would have preferred the hot genie delivering my desires without any effort, but I had to do some work on myself first. I had to do one of the hardest things of all, which was to change my thinking.

During those dark early days when I feared for my sanity, I constantly read books to bolster my belief, consuming every classic in the field I could lay my hands on. They had hokey titles like *The Amazing Laws of Cosmic Mind Power* and *Your Word is Your Wand.* For the most part I limited myself to books written by dead people because the cynical part of my mind wouldn't allow me to buy new books on the subject: "Sure, anyone can get rich telling people they can get rich by doing nothing but reading their books."

The classics came with their own set of problems. Published at the dawn of the New Thought movement, the sexism contained in their pages was by turns quaint and alarming. The authors would go on and on about how "You gents" can make a million bucks or even be President with the consciousness of wealth and success!...Oh, and "You gals" can get a new set of dishes, a fox stole, or even a wealthy husband.

Still, what I loved about them was their forthrightness, their simplicity, their absolute conviction. Cynicism had been my biggest obstacle to achieving happiness and I had to find a way out from under its crushing weight. What helped me was reading those wonderful, unabashedly hopeful books.

One agent who turned down this manuscript said she couldn't tell whether it was a memoir, a book on writing, or a metaphysical how-to book. It's all three, a hybrid. I wrote it as a testimonial like the New Thought classics, only more contemporary.

Mine is not a Cinderella story. That's where the "short of Nirvana" bit comes in. I'm not a famous author (not that I'm ruling it out in the future); nor am I anybody's idea of a guru. I'm still working hard on all of this but I didn't want to wait until I was high on a mountaintop to share these principles with you. For one thing, I have a morbid fear of mountain roads.

In chapter 13 I talk about a monkey-see, monkey-do phenomenon I call a "miracle contagion," an idea supported by the discovery of mirror neurons in the human brain. The theory goes that once you see one of your species engaged in a new activity, it sparks the same ability in you.

It's my ambition to set off a miracle contagion in my readers. Please get in touch with me and let me know what happens to you after reading this book. If you'd like to jump ahead and see what I mean by miracles you can turn to page 44 where I define my terms. I look forward to hearing all about your successes at the Big-Ass Miracles Café online!

PART I

A Heavenly Vision

"Is that you, God?

Or is it low blood sugar?

Seeing isn't always Believing

I was around twenty years old when I first saw God.

But enough about me. How are *you* doing?

Okay, I'm understandably shy when it comes to talking about my vision. I will relate the story only if you promise not to think me completely unhinged. After all, this book *is sort of* a memoir, my life as a travelogue through Weirdsville, and I'd be remiss if I didn't include the event that sent me hurtling down its proverbial Main Street.

Nor would I want to sneak up on you with it. What a cheap trick that would be—reminiscing about walking at the age of one, learning what the potty was for at two, tying my own Keds for the first time at three, meandering through my childhood in suburban Dallas as the middle child of four, with a lawyer for a father and a musician mother, and then going off to college at seventeen to study foreign languages so I could get the hell out of Texas, when—

WHAM.

I hit you with a God sighting.

The problem is that's exactly how it happened.

My family was Presbyterian, a religion so low-key as to seem almost apologetic. My church memories are of a man in a black robe making unfunny golf jokes from the pulpit, singing dead-boring hymns from a musty, maroon-colored book, drinking *faux* communion wine that was supposed to represent the blood sacrifice of Christ—who I'm guessing did not actually bleed grape juice—and asking to be forgiven for our sins before adjourning to the gym, where the adults would swap business cards over coffee and donut holes. It was where we kids were obliged to sit in a circle while the Sunday school teacher talked about places that might as well have been on the moon, like "Judea" and "Babylon."

I loved Jesus (what's not to love?) but I hated church. During the sermons I fantasized about leaping off the choir loft and swinging out on the brass chandeliers over the congregation yodeling like Tarzan. One time I sincerely offered to do all of the dishes for the rest of my life if my mother would let me quit going. She didn't accept my offer, but I still ended up doing the dishes.

Mom was tricky that way. Always one step ahead of us kids. I never knew how she did it, until one day I was rooting around in the study and found a black book with the words *Child Psychology* stamped on it in gold.

That's how she always knew what we were up to. I vowed to read lots and lots of hardcover books when I grew up. All power would then be mine.

Even as a kid, I was a voracious reader, always with my nose in a book. Books entertained me, took me to far-flung locales, thrilled me, taught me things about the world. It was through books that I learned why George was so curious, how it felt to be tiny and airborne like Thumbelina, and most pertinent to my later life, how to escape the ever-present peril facing a girl detective like Nancy Drew.

Mom wanted me to be a musician. Although I tried to please her, I ended up breaking her heart when I quit the piano after ten long years of lessons. Music wasn't my language. I didn't hear it speak the way real musicians did. It was always my goal to be a writer.

My early efforts won praise, starting with an epic poem I wrote about my tonsillectomy at six: "Tonsils are as grey as they can be/ But the doctor said mine looked like green cottage cheese." I went on to describe my kidnapping in the middle of the procedure by Martians. (So I *embellished* a little.)

In the fourth grade, I wrote illustrated books featuring a family of pigs with long eyelashes and bows on their ears. My art teacher, Mrs. King, convinced Mom that I should be writing children's books for real, then she took me out of the class and sat me up at the front of the room in full view of everyone to write my masterpieces. I froze, no longer able to conjure a single talking animal from my imagination. The project was quietly dropped.

That didn't stop me from writing. Storytelling was in my blood. One of my favorite pastimes was making up horror stories to tell my little cousin under the covers at our grandmother's house, freaking her out with The Killer Washing Machine that trapped unwary kids and tumble-dried them to death, along with other hair-raising tales.

It was in college that I got my first paying gig. I received the princely sum of twenty dollars for ghost writing an essay on Franz Kafka's *Metamorphosis*. The jock I authored it for got an A, but also the unwanted attention of the professor, who handed it back to him with the words *I like the way you challenge the critics* scrawled across the top.

The professor spent the rest of the semester trying to corner the poor guy to discuss his ideas. I'd argued that Gregor Samsa's cockroach was not a metaphor, but an actual genetic mutation that could happen in real life. Perhaps the prof had wanted to steer my friend toward the campus mental health clinic.

For my playwriting course I wrote an absurdist one-act, a paean to Ionesco. What I really wanted to do was write screenplays or novels, but there were no course offerings for those. That didn't concern me. I had the rest of my life to figure it out. One reason I was anxious to leave Texas was so I could rack up some amazing life experiences to explore in the pages of a book. I mean, how could you be the next Lillian Hellman or Dalton Trumbo unless you'd really lived?

Before I could make a start, soaring out of the nest with the wind at my back, there was an unwanted experience in the form of a tragedy. Fall semester of my second year, I got the call to come home.

The End of the Women

*M*om had always suffered from migraines. The doctor put this down to being a "high strung gal." *Relax, have a Bloody Mary. Go buy yourself a new dress.*

In the end, it was a cerebral cyst that killed her, *not* her feminine nerves. She'd been knocked out with a headache for ten days when my father returned from work to find her unresponsive in bed. Only weeks before that she'd made the rounds, visiting me, my brother, and my older sister at our respective colleges.

I think she knew.

I'd been so proud to introduce her to my friends. Everyone agreed that my mother was cool. I especially enjoyed sitting in the dorm room chatting with her into the wee hours like a couple of coeds. We spoke frankly about issues like sex and boys and marriage, laughing and having a great old time. I'd been looking forward to this new kind of relationship with her, one between equals, but it wasn't to be.

While she lay in the hospital, I slept twelve hours a day, trying to blot out the image of my pretty mother hooked up to all that machinery, bloated beyond recognition. Then one afternoon we gathered under a shade tree on the hospital grounds to make the hardest decision anyone ever has to make. I felt as if I were floating outside myself, watching my family members groping for words like a troupe of actors who'd forgotten their scripts. I can't actually recall taking part in the discussion of whether to cut off life support, but I must have cast a vote. At any rate, it was done.

It's safe to say I didn't believe in miracles at the time. Like any educated American, I'd placed my faith in the people manning those machines, reading those electronic outputs, wielding those needles, prescribing those pills. If they said there was no hope, who was I to disagree? With what authority, what science to back me up? I didn't pray for Mom's recovery. Her death was a medical certainty.

My father forbade us to cry at the funeral. We stood in a receiving line in the elegant, red-carpeted sanctuary of the church, the widower and his well-disciplined brood, greeting the mourners with soldierly stoicism. It might have been a wedding or a graduation ceremony for all the grief we displayed. My mother's friends, on the other hand, wept like banshees. I almost felt sorrier for them than I did for myself.

The preacher said something I'd always remember. He said that Mom loved her children so much she let them go free, knowing they'd always come back. Pardon me, but exactly how were we supposed to do that now? Throw ourselves into the grave with her? I didn't want to be free of her permanently.

Her death wasn't just devastating, it was *wrong*. Your mother was supposed to guide you through womanhood as your best friend and confidante, to be there for the milestones, your wedding and the birth of your children. Especially when she had *promised* to. Once as a kid, I begged her to quit smoking—they'd told us how dangerous it was at school—but she only laughed. "I'll be around just as long as you need me," she assured me'

Again, it wasn't the cigarettes that killed her, but some deadly depth charge God had planted in her brain.

Even though I loathed church, secretly I'd always been God's girl. My parents used to call family meetings during which they'd read a passage from the Bible, one that just happened to deal the issue of obedience. It turned out that God really, really wanted children to obey their parents. He even insisted, on pain of—actually, that went unsaid, but I could read between the lines. There was a hot, fiery hell for kids who disobeyed.

I sat there like a novice taking her vows, rapt with attention, swearing to uphold the holy writ. While my siblings continued tussling and biting each other, I was off in my head

thinking: *I shall obey my parents and thereby find favor with my Father in Heaven, forever and ever, Amen.*[*]

---

[*] When asked if they remembered these impromptu Bible lessons, they've all responded in the negative. It appears I was the only one who bought into the whole thing.

In addition to being a good girl, I prayed every night for God to keep my loved ones safe. Maybe I'd become a bit lax in adolescence—shall we chalk that up to hormones? I always *meant* to stay in touch. Was that any reason for such harsh treatment?

Did the punishment fit the crime, here?

I didn't curse God when Mom died. What would be the point? He was obviously a sadistic bastard who liked to mislead little kids into believing they would get what they prayed for, pulling the rug out from under them afterward. Showing how much it hurt would give Him that much more pleasure. You don't give someone such an incredible mother only to snatch her back so soon. Not unless it was your diabolical plan all along.

Yes, I'd once been God's little sucker. Now all bets were off.

My father was at a complete loss—nothing had prepared him for this. A decorated veteran, he'd survived five major military campaigns, including the Normandy Invasion. If he could live through mortar attacks and bullet and shrapnel wounds and dysentery and knife fights with German soldiers, how could death sneak in and take his cherished wife from the safety of her own bed?

After the funeral, we older kids broke camp, leaving our younger sister with an absentee father and a credit card. I'm still haunted by that, but I was too numb and emotionally unschooled to help. There were only a couple of years between us.

And so I returned to San Antonio to lose myself in my studies. My university was a small one with only three thousand students. When you were out, you were missed. The German professor asked me *auf Deutsch* where I'd been, and I realized I had a choice in responding. There are two verbs in German for getting sick. One implies that the person has recovered; the other, not.

Being an A student, I used the correct verb: "Meine Mutter *got sick and died.*"

The professor thought I'd made a typical mistake. "You mean your Mutter *got sick but now she's fine,*" he corrected me, using the verb with the happier ending.

I sat there as long as I could with my paternally mandated stiff upper lip, then I burst into tears and ran from the room. The poor man looked stricken at his mistake.

At least I'd finally managed to cry.

This period became known as The End of the Women, a prelude to The End of the Men a decade and a half later. Now I believe that there are worse things than dying—losing your soul, for one—but at the time I was very attached to life and the people in it. Three such losses in a row were extremely hard to take.

My best childhood friend had been killed months earlier in a car accident. We'd grown apart in our teens but she'd already shaped my character by then. If I'm wacky, it's because Andrea McNiel made me that way. Although she deserves her own book, I'll sum her up by saying she was hilarious and a criminal genius—Huck Finn to my Tom Sawyer. When I met her college boyfriend he told me he'd only recently managed to hook up with her after months of ardent pursuit. The reason she gave? "If I die in a car crash tomorrow, I don't want to die a virgin."

Two down, one to go.

Now, what would you do for an encore if you were the God of the Old Testament, that nasty bearded guy who went around smiting people and siccing whales on them and asking them to decapitate their sons just to appease you? What could you possibly do that would top taking someone's beloved mother and her best childhood friend within the space of a few months?

I know, I'll kill her little dog, too!

My brother accidentally ran over our wired-hair terrier, Sunday, in the driveway. He'd found her as a puppy on his paper route, which is how she got her name. I'll never forget the sight of him weeping over her fuzzy little tan and white carcass, wracked with guilt.

Well.

That was a fun trip down Memory Lane, wasn't it?

Perhaps you can understand now why I was hell-bent on getting away from there. And why, if there was a God, he wasn't my favorite person. Also, why God was the last thing I expected to see on that particular day...

3

"Pi" in the Sky

I'd long since stopped practicing any sort of faith. There was no flagellating myself with a whip or prostrating myself on a cold monastery floor; no hint of religious ecstasy, only grinding boredom. I was tabulating some statistics with nary a spiritual thought in my head, when all of a sudden—

An explosion of light invaded my consciousness, shutting out the world around me and lighting up my mind from within.

I'm aware of how one's own epiphanies sound like idiocies to others. They reek of marijuana, like a stoner's discovery that the word "God" is actually "dog" spelled backwards. I can't help that. It was my experience and all I can do is relate it honestly.

To earn money for a semester abroad, I was interning at my father's office. On this occasion I'd been sent to toil at another firm that was supporting him on a big case. They'd given me a makeshift workspace, a converted utility closet containing an old wooden desk, with no natural light or ventilation, and only a bare light bulb hanging overhead. It was a great place to spend eight hours a day, if you were a mop. My assignment was to tally employees for an exhibit to be used in a case of employee discrimination.

Anyway, I was shut away without light or air, and I happen to have been on a liquid diet that was popular at the time, trying to lose the extra weight I'd gained pounding nachos and Dr. Pepper in the student lounge. This miracle elixir was neon pink and viscous, kind of like runny Jell-O. It was later recalled by the Food and Drug Administration; whether that was for producing unsolicited visions of God, I cannot say.

You were supposed to choke down the tasteless goo for breakfast and lunch, and then eat a proper dinner—although I may have been skipping dinner too. It was to this dubious diet regimen that I initially attributed what happened to me that afternoon:

There was a cracking sound in my head. Actually, it was more like a ripping. Above me flashed a mathematical equation spreading out across the sky. I call it the sky because the backdrop to the equation was a strip of white, shining clouds. Also, it was so high up in the atmosphere that I must somehow have been viewing it *through* the ceiling of the stuffy closet.

It was bright and immense and astounding.

Despite its complexity I somehow understood it. I don't mean I could have solved it as a math problem, but I knew that something was being communicated to me beyond a set of numbers and symbols. Precisely because it was infinite, it could never be solved, and wasn't meant to be. You could never get your mind around the whole thing.

Strange as this sounds, seeing it gave me a feeling of comfort, of certitude about my place in the universe.

I didn't seek it.

It appeared.

It couldn't be "understood."

It simply was.

And best of all, I sensed that the author of the equation saw me.

Knew me.

Immediately on the heels of that indescribably magnificent, mind-bending experience came the thought:

"Holy Ding Dongs, Batman. I'd better eat something."

Complaining of a headache, I left the office for the day, laying down tracks to the nearest hamburger stand. The vision had lasted only a couple of seconds, but that was enough to hurl me into a state of uncertainty.

Had I seen God? Or had I suffered a stroke?

We have a cultural expectation of what happens as a result of illumination. The person is transformed into a sage or Buddha. He has pierced the veil of illusion, never to return to ordinary stunted consciousness again. He then goes on to becomes a prophet or teacher, a bearer of light for the rest of humanity.

If that's the way it's *supposed* to go then my illumination may have been a bit, *um*, premature. I had my God moment, then was off and running again on the hamster wheel of fortune, never slowing to consider its meaning. I ran to Paris and Hollywood and Delhi, and various parts in between. Was I running away from the experience, or toward it?

It doesn't matter. You can run, but there's nowhere to hide from God.

It's only after the reading of many, many spiritual books, and after meditating for many years that I am prepared to view that experience as a profound, life-changing event. Only now can I see it not merely as the product of a glucose-starved brain—although that may have set the stage, like the visions of self-denying saints of yore—but as a gift from some higher intelligence.

Why, you ask, *would anyone equate a set of numbers and symbols with the Supreme Being?*

I answer that question with, *Why not?*

Perhaps God represents in a way that is meaningful to the experiencer at any given point in time. To a nomad in 1500 B.C.E., God took on the appearance of a burning bush or a talking goat. In twentieth-century America a mathematical equation might have seemed a more appropriate guise.[*]

---

[*] I may have made up the goat part. I haven't memorized the *whole* Bible.

For me this was a whole new way of perceiving the Divine Spirit. Not as that whimsical, mentally unstable punisher in the sky, but as Infinite Intelligence.

The question that can probably never be resolved is this:

Are we capable of seeing God in any form?

If we insist that we have, must there be some physical or psychological aberration to account for it? A tumor pressing on the optic nerve? A hysterical, fantasy-prone personality? A borderline anorectic suffering the effects of a fad diet?

If it was a hallucination brought on by low blood sugar, then why doesn't every dieter have the same experience? I can attest that Slim-Fast never brought on such a vision. Neither did Atkins, Fit for Life, The Zone, or Ten Years Thinner. They all had their high points—dried skin, bruising, hair loss, hunger, sometimes even weight reduction—but illumination never figured into it.

Even people who like to toss off the phrase, *The Lord works in mysterious ways* would probably look at me askance and say, "Not *that* mysterious."

I console myself with a quote by Martin Luther King:

"It's the cracked ones who let in the light."

Perhaps you have to jump off the rails in order to get an idea of the enormity of God. Even a split-second glimpse can cause you to doubt your sanity.

So much has happened between that time and this. A lot of cracks, a little light. If that had been my only hint of the Infinite, a one-time peek behind the curtain, I might have left it there. But I seem to have been destined to make the long, difficult journey from hardened cynic to autodidact mystic, from *what-you-see-is-what-you-get* pragmatist to Miracle Mama.

You know what they say about drinking—that as long as it's working for you, you won't think about quitting? At that time of my life, youth, energy, and unfocused ambition were working as handily as any brew. Eventually I would need another way of being but I wouldn't see that until I had no other choice.

Nevertheless, once I became desperate enough to suspend my skepticism, I experienced what I now consider to be divine guidance. I've learned that the left side of the brain—the analytical side—has to be placed in abeyance when attempting to connect with the Divine. You have to tell it to sit down and shut up when you embark on your spiritual journey, because analyzing God is like trying to read in the dark wearing sunglasses.

As for me, I'd remain in the dark for a long time to come.

PART II

Hooray for Hollywood!

"How I sold my soul to the
Devil and got squat in return."

4

Merchant of Shattered Dreams

"This is not my beautiful life!"

—The Talking Heads

*F*ast-forward to Los Angeles in 1997.

Which finds me sitting on the back patio of my friend's Century City duplex, wondering where it all went wrong. Two years after being married on two separate continents, my husband and I have split up. I'm broke, unemployed, and virtually unemployable (bad attitude, no useful skills), totally jaded about the entertainment business I've worked in for fifteen years, to say nothing of my own life.

What happened?

At twenty-five I'd arrived in Hollywood like a dazzled Dorothy landing in Oz. Since then there'd been good times and bum times, boyfriends and broken engagements, and one demanding job after the other but no success in my desired field. Now the shine was definitely off the penny. Emerald City was a factory town like any other.

Throughout those years, I'd always written scripts on the side. Before the advent of the laptop I'd come home from the office or work trips to crank out screenplays on an old Apple III. Nights and weekends you'd find me there, pounding away at the dining room table. Sometimes with a partner; usually, alone.

There'd been some encouragement—positive reader coverage, a win in a competition at the American Film Institute, various nibbles and close calls from producers—but no cigar in the form of paying work.

Trying to keep it up while being an executive was brutal. Many times I thought about running a Laundromat or driving a taxi to give me more peace of mind, more time to write. Instead, I continued to rise through the ranks, becoming a VP of Children's Programming at LIVE Entertainment.

It was hard not to be seduced by the new success of the company I'd worked at for four years. Once a vaguely sleazy video business with a pornographer at the helm, it had morphed into an up and coming independent with an impressive slate of releases and the latest entertainment darling of Wall Street. The credit for this was all due to the recently installed CEO, a former Hertz executive by the name of Jose Menendez.

One reason I'd stuck around was that my colleague Richard Gladstein had undertaken to produce one of my scripts. *The Catch* was a black comedy about a woman who marries an old and ailing millionaire for his money, who then refuses to die (with riotous results). The production company was Neo Films, whose lead partner made a name for himself with *Bill and Ted's Excellent Adventure.*

Robert Ellis Miller (*Reuben, Reuben*) was attached to direct. *Young Frankenstein's* Teri Garr had committed to playing the lead role. LIVE would provide the financing in exchange for worldwide rights. At long last, it appeared all of my efforts would pay off.

In August of 1989, the VP of Sales had a Sunday barbecue at his home in the San Fernando Valley. It was a fun, relaxing party full of good food, drink, and camaraderie. For some reason, Jose and his wife Kitty were no-shows. This was surprising, as Jose was big on company solidarity. We all assumed that he'd had some business to attend to, but the reality was something very different.

The next day I was calling in to make some excuse for playing hooky, when my boss's assistant, Lynn, told me in a choked whisper that Jose and Kitty had been murdered.

I threw the phone across the room. Somehow, I ended up on the floor. After a few stunned moments, I realized I'd left Lynn hanging and picked up the receiver, shivering as if from an Arctic blast of air.

While she recounted the details of the murders, I blinked and shook my head, trying to make sense out of it. *Jose and Kitty, gunned down in their mansion? How could this be? Beverly Hills is one of the safest cities in the world!* I even had a momentary, irrational fear that I would be a suspect because I was calling in sick.

Murder does strange things to your head.

For weeks everyone at the company walked around in a zombified state, waiting for someone to be arrested. The gangland-style killing bore the taint of a scandal, making it catnip for the tabloids. Tantalized by the sordidness of the crime, people called up demanding the dirt. It was like being kicked back into a gutter that you'd only just managed to crawl out of.

Not knowing who had done it left the constitutionally paranoid among us—*me*—feeling very afraid. It would be some time before Jose's sons came under suspicion, transforming the murder mystery into a Greek tragedy. Their motive centered on alleged sexual abuse, but who will ever know?

The company offered a single grief counseling session in the break room. I found myself sitting around the table with only three co-workers out of a couple of hundred. It sounds terrible, but many of my colleagues were conflicted over the death of Jose, who was known for his harsh and sometimes bullying treatment of employees. It's hard to empathize with bullies even when they've been brutally killed.

Jose had always reminded me of my dad—smart and tough-minded, with a disarming sense of humor. They even resembled one another, like variations on Orson Welles. Both men could really turn on the charm. And both could be really mean.

Around that time in Dallas, Pop was succumbing to cirrhosis. Already emotional because of this, I broke down at the meeting, crying for Jose and Kitty, for myself, for my father, but most of all for those poor orphaned boys. It's strange now to think now that I actually identified with Lyle and Erik.

Rumors began to circulate about their involvement. In the hallways people gathered to discuss this theory of the murders. *Was it possible the boys were that ruthless?* I recalled seeing Lyle in the building for the first time, asking someone about the cute guy I'd seen talking on the phone near Jose's office. When I was told who he was, I'd yelped and run in the opposite direction.

I found the boys to be self-possessed and charming. Maybe a little cocky, but that comes with the territory when you're young, rich, and handsome. They seemed to have inherited Jose's intelligence, too. It looked like they were headed for great things.

Great notoriety, as it turned out.

After Jose's death, our stock tanked, the management changed, things were never really the same at LIVE. Richard left to produce *Pulp Fiction* for Miramax. *The Catch* never got made.

The company bounced back within a year; it took me a lot longer. Can you ever really "bounce back" from the shotgun slaying of someone you knew and admired?

Perhaps, but only with deep emotional scarring. Never again would I feel quite the same level of optimism or safety as before it happened, and it wasn't even to be the end of the troubles.

5

The End of the Men

*A*s Pop lay dying in the hospital that summer, my siblings and I accompanied our stepmother back and forth from the family home in Dallas to his bedside. He was a shadow of his former burly self. Breathing tube down the throat, hands pierced by IV needles, wrists strapped to the bedrails.

The foot soldier who fathered four children, who'd camped out in a pup tent at the University of Texas while he earned his law degree then built a name for himself in the legal profession, who played left-handed golf and tennis tournaments and been a jogger and a devoted gardener, but who never really got over the death of my mother (apologies to my stepmother), had simply left the building. All that remained was a withered husk, like a beetle's carapace shed on the sidewalk.

Watching the dissipation of my father, and still reeling from the Menendez murders, I was sinking into fatalism.

This is it, then? We are born to stumble around blind and miserable until at last we call it quits, only to be kept hanging on in even worse misery?

Say it ain't so, I thought. *Tell me it's possible to have some happiness and joy, a smidge of laughter and even a little love between the cradle and the grave. Don't let this be what life is.*

My father lasted until January.

Jose had been murdered the previous August.

There followed two more deaths in quick succession. This time the bad news came in fours instead of threes.

My beloved uncle, Pop's brother, succumbed to throat cancer soon after Pop died. I'm sure that a lingering feud between the two of them hastened his demise.

Then my maternal grandfather, the only surviving member of the family in south Texas, died at the age of ninety-four.

According to the nurse he was carrying on an animated conversation with a ceramic angel when he passed. I really wanted to believe there was a scintillating winged creature in that room beckoning him to the big back porch in the sky, where he could smoke his pipe in a rocking chair and chortle at the cartoons in the newspaper for all eternity.

Was there anything after this life? Was this just a jumping off place for something grander? My stepmother told us that a second after Pop died, he snapped back to attention and grasped her hand, looking as if he wanted to tell her something about where he'd just been.

He didn't have time before he slipped away again.

It sometimes felt that there would be no end to the funerals, and it will probably come as no surprise that I tried to escape the pain by creating escapist entertainment.

6

Operator, get me Jesus on the Line

*S*o there I was living in my friend's Century City duplex, where I was renting a room for $300 a month, suspended while I tried to get back on my feet. A business deal had just fallen through, leaving me with no alternative but to declare bankruptcy. If I was adrift before, now I was completely lost.

No clue had I as to what to do next. [*Ed. – I told her to stop beginning all her sentences with the word "I."*] Too embarrassed was I to ask anyone for a job, and too traumatized by my professional spiral to reinvent myself as an executive—which I'd never wanted to be in the first place—and too freaked out by the total cratering of my life at forty to envision a way out.

How do you reassemble the pieces of a broken life? Is there some cosmic glue that can repair it without visible cracks? Or is it a better idea to put the pieces into a blender and grind them into a fine powder, tossing it into the wind to start over from scratch?

My pieces were not about to submit to a gluing. They no longer fit together in any meaningful way. Suspecting that I'd been wrong about the very fundamentals of existence, that perhaps there *was* more to this life than consuming and striving and trying to look good doing it...

I set out to discover what that elusive something was.[*]

Having done so poorly on my own, I decided it was time to revisit my friend the Equation. Though agnostic, I would throw myself open to whatever might come my way. If there *was* a God, he was going to by god help me in my time of need.

The only question was, what procedure should I follow? Should I get down on my knees and fold my hands in prayer?

No, too corny. If there is a God, He's omniscient, He'll see right through that.

Instead I started a journal called "Listening to God," which really should have been called "Screeching *at* God." Essentially it was a series of letters addressed to the alleged Almighty. Here's an excerpt from the very first journal entry, cut down from six pages:

Ltg 12-29-97

Okay, I think I'll start a journal, because I'm so conflicted and so troubled. It's time to stop going to outside people: doctors, shrinks, gurus, etc., because I must have the answer to my own anguish. If not me, then who?

---

[*] Sometimes you have to put yourself at the beginning of the sentence.

I feel friendless, I feel desperate financially. I feel hopeless about my relationship with Rajeev. I don't know what to do about having kids. I'm so unhappy. . .

Please help me to get stronger. Please help me to find and keep joy and love in my heart. Please help me to live in gratitude for every day.

I'm so afraid. So afraid. So afraid.

Are you reminded of that girl in *The Blair Witch Project* who bawls into the camera with her nose running like a spigot? Sorry, but you need the context for everything that follows. I will include these journal entries from time to time to show exactly what I was thinking as I went about rebuilding my life, providing a real-time chronicle of my hopes and fears, along with the prayers I used to combat the terror.

Eventually, the writing helped me to cope with my new situation. The more I gave voice to my worries, the less potent they seemed to be. And after a while, I realized that my one-way conversation was becoming a two-way conversation. God indeed had a message for me:

Get over yourself, my child.

Get over your idea of who you thought you were, get over what you thought you were owed in this life, get over all of your "broken dreams" and your disappointments and get *out there and start over.*

First on the agenda: cash. I needed food in the belly and gas in the tank. A friend had begun working at a temp agency when his advertising company failed. He was a former VP with good people skills, and had landed a fulltime job at Spelling Entertainment.

When he offered to recommend me to the agency, I was terror-struck. How competent would I be at performing basic office functions? If I sucked, could I use the excuse of having had assistants of my own until very recently?

Probably not.

Nevertheless, he called the agency on my behalf, I took the tests, passed them somehow, and was hired.

My maiden voyage was at Paramount Pictures, working for an elderly producer whose office was plastered with posters from all of his big movies. *This could be interesting*, I thought, never having worked with a big studio producer before. I soon discovered just how interesting it could be working for a one-time movie mogul who was suffering from Alzheimer's.

He occupied office space that was off the studio lot, but his overhead was still covered—either through charity or through a long-standing deal with no exit clause. I thought he was a cute old codger at first, but soon realized what I'd gotten myself into. His wife dropped him off every morning around ten, then he'd spend the day behind a large desk cutting coupons and talking to himself. Every once in a while he'd call me into his office, giving me a gimlet-eyed look, and ask me where his checkbook was.

When I'd go looking for it in his desk drawer, he'd shout, "It's not there! It's not there! Where *is* it?"

How did I get here? This is not my beautiful job, God!

I was sure the man's wife had hidden his checkbook along with his car keys, but how could I say that to him? Starting out my new life being accused as a thief was probably not ideal. I bowed out of that assignment as quickly as possible.

The next assignment was at a property management company in downtown LA. That's what I was doing when my roommate threw a July 4th barbecue.

Trying to act more sociable than I felt, I helped her get ready for the party, setting the table, chilling the wine, slicing zucchini and tomatoes, marinating chicken for the grill. It was a beautiful day, with her hanging baskets of colorful impatiens in full bloom. My friend's white German shepherd lay sprawled on the green grass, stuffed with the deviled eggs she'd stolen from a serving tray when our backs were turned.

One of my roommate's coworkers, a young guy named Jeff, showed up at the celebration. While we were chatting, he mentioned that he had started attending a church with a metaphysical slant. It was called the Los Angeles Church of Religious Science[*] (LACRS), and was housed in a fabulous old Art Deco theater on Wilshire Boulevard.

Jeff was so funny and cute, so totally normal-looking with his stylish brown haircut and big blue eyes—he was the furthest thing from a religious nut I could imagine. And he didn't seem to be proselytizing, just telling me how much he was

---

[*] *Not* to be confused with Scientology. No extraterrestrial cooties in this tradition.

helped by the church's teaching. If he said there was something of value in this metaphysical business, it might be true.

"Maybe I'll try it," I said, ever the smart ass. "I'm always in the market for a new religion."

Tip: Start a journal, stating what you want out of life.

This is the beginning of a dialog between you and You. Tell your journal exactly what's on your mind. Don't hold back.

Don't worry about sounding like a whiney jerk, and don't fret about wanting too much. Nobody (with the exception of the entire Universe) will be eavesdropping on your private thoughts.

When you write down your fears and concerns, along with your hopes and dreams, it's as if your conscious mind (you) begins speaking to your *expanded* mind (You = you + the Divine Mind). This is the part of you that knows how to fix things. Once it sees what you want, it will put you into situations and places, cause you to run into people who are on your wavelength, bring you books and downloads, whatever you need to get your life back on course.

You've heard the expression "When the student is ready, the teacher appears."

Well, writing this stuff down is like blasting the instructor out of the teacher's lounge with an announcement that break time is over and *this kid is ready for class.*

End Tip

PART III

Meditation, miracles,

writing career

"Finally, I get a clue!"

Miracles

(n. *p.* Méer-a-cullz)

1) Things that should not have been, but were, 2) things you couldn't have known, but did, 3) freaky coincidences that can't be explained, try though you might, 4) prayers that have been answered directly, 5) physical feats that were impossible but did somehow occur, 6) unexpected healings, 7) other weird stuff, to be defined as I go along.

7

Show Tunes for the Spiritually Impaired

My flippancy with Jeff was disingenuous. I really did want some kind of spiritual practice but there wasn't a single religion on the planet I felt I could relate to.

Later that week he dropped off a copy of *Creative Thought* magazine, a publication distributed through the Church of Religious Science (now the Centers for Spiritual Living). On the cover of the magazine was a photo of singer Naomi Judd, looking radiantly healthy after her bout with Hepatitis C. (You may recall that she retired from performing on account of the liver illness, which is believed to be a slow killer.)

It turned out that the unsinkable Ms. Judd took neither her diagnosis nor her prognosis lying down. After going on a special diet, taking natural supplements, and practicing meditation, she defied the medical community and its dire predictions by showing up a couple of years later, completely C-free.

Could this be believed? Perhaps the doctors had misdiagnosed her in the first place. There was no blood work offered in the magazine to support her story, no doctor's reports from before or after the amazing healing. Despite my knee-jerk skepticism, something in me desperately wanted to believe that such miracles were possible. I'd seen people die in very ugly ways, and it would be nice to think that illness could be so gracefully cured.

Physical ailments weren't the only thing susceptible to mental healing, according to this teaching. It could ameliorate depression, improve finances, repair broken relationships, heal the whole host of human ills, psychological, emotional, and financial. They made the startling claim that *all* such problems were of a spiritual origin.

Naomi's case was one of many that had stumped the experts. I had to know more about this, even though a little voice in my head was screaming—*Look out, it's a cult!*

My sisters certainly feared as much when I started attending services on a regular basis. One of my father's favorite comedy bits had always been Flip Wilson's spoof of New Age religion, "The Church of What's Happenin' Now."

Was Pop turning over in his military grave?

Still, the place appeared to be just what it said it was—a house of God, albeit with a different slant on things and a different congregation from the kind I was used to in Dallas. My old church is in the neighborhood where George W. Bush now hangs his Stetson, which should tell you everything. The services at LACRS took place on Sunday mornings and were attended by well dressed people who sang songs, listened to a sermon, and then passed a plate. Pretty churchy, right? They were members of the International Council of Churches and no one had ever tried to revoke their tax-exempt status. They didn't ask me to sell flowers on street corners and there wasn't a saffron robe to be seen.

Being a film buff, I loved attending services in a grand old movie palace. Now instead of Tarzan fantasies, I could imagine Clark Gable sitting in the seat next to mine, laughing at a screening of *It Happened One Night* with his hand on Carole Lombard's knee. Whenever I got restless, I leaned back to admire the geometric designs on the ceiling, or the glowing triangular wall sconces. The upholstery was plush, the flower arrangements fresh, and the music was *great*. Many of the members were performers eager to sing on Sunday mornings.

There were also a lot of film and TV actors in the congregation. I'll never forget the morning when they called a woman named Esther Williams to the stage. *Poor thing*, I thought, *going through life with that name! How many times has she been asked, "You wearing a bathing suit under that dress, yuk, yuk?"*

However, when the woman walked up on stage, she actually *was* Esther Williams.

The preacher, Dr. Walker, was also a far cry from the black-robed, unfunny preachers of my youth. He was a tall man with white hair, a wide girth, red cheeks, and feet that just had to dance. I especially appreciated the way he'd break out into song during his sermons: "The Man in the Moon is a *Laaaaady*."

Though he was truly hilarious, he could be thoughtful and dignified, too, and was at all times a wonderful teacher.

The philosophy was derived from the New Thought movement of the late nineteenth and early twentieth centuries, notable for thinkers like Ralph Waldo Emerson and Judge Thomas Troward. The Bible was still the Bible, but interpretation was in line with Ernest Holmes's book *The Science of Mind*. The main point of the teaching was that "thoughts are things," the building blocks of reality. What you hold in consciousness will determine your experience in life.

I returned every week, sitting in the balcony by myself and dropping money into the collection bag after the service as if leaving a tip on my way out the door. I purchased my own copy of *The Science of Mind,* removing the cover when I read the book at the Laundromat for fear of being taken for a whacko. Why I imagined anyone would care, I cannot say. [*Ed.– Remember, this is the woman who thought she'd be the prime suspect in the Menendez murders.*]

Maybe I thought God was looking over my shoulder and wouldn't approve. Even though I was an adult, the idea of a punishing God was still lodged in my brain from childhood. The tenets of this religion seemed very "out there" to me, while at the same time resonating with something deep inside, a sense I'd always had about the way things *should* be.

Instead of calling us unworthy worms of the dust, Dr. Walker told us we were the earthly incarnations of God. The word "sin" was spoken of as an archery term, meaning "missing the mark." He taught that Jesus was not the great exception but the great example; we could all learn to heal and bless one another. Ernest Holmes even went so far as to claim it was possible for all people to perform miracles if they "prayed aright."

The underlying assumption is that our minds are part of the greater Mind of God, participating in the act of creation rather than existing apart from it. And being connected to all things, we have the power to affect the outer world.

It took some serious cranial rewiring to accept these ideas on a conscious level, but my heart leapt at them eagerly.

I would later learn that this line of thinking is supported by cutting-edge science. The concept of *interconnectivity* is one of the main principles of quantum physics, which has confirmed that once a subatomic particle has been entangled with (or connected to) another particle, the two remain in contact no matter how far apart they may travel, influencing the behavior of one another across space and even across time.

At the most fundamental level of existence, there is no separation. There is an invisible essence that connects all things.

This quantum stuff or Infinite Intelligence is represented in all religions, alternately referred to as the Holy spirit, consciousness, Brahma, the Divine Mind, the Zero Point Field—take your pick. *It* certainly doesn't care what you call it. Those of the *Star Wars* generation might prefer The Force.

It's in me. It's in you. It's the source of all creation, and it continues to create on a second-to-second basis.

Meditation, I learned, was the way to interact with this divine essence. Practicing daily, I would tell myself I was "going where God is" in order to get into the zone. First I would slow my breathing, while trying to stop the mental chatter in my head. Then I let myself sink into a state where my mind felt suspended in cotton and my body was as light as air and cocooned in calm. It's when you're floating in this mental spaciousness—this "non-ordinary state of awareness"—that you're able to access the quantum realm and affect your life.

It's also the place where you can receive guidance.

The study of metaphysics began chipping away at my feelings of isolation, of being the victim of circumstance. It was no longer possible to think of things happening in a haphazard fashion. There was no such thing as "luck," good or bad. Dr. Gary Schwartz, an author and professor at the University of Arizona, had this to say on the subject:

"The conditions for randomness do not exist in our universe."

In order for things to be random they would have to occur in a vacuum, completely unaffected by their surroundings. Quantum entanglement renders this impossible. Everything is *a continuation of* everything else—there's no dividing line to be found.

When looked at this way, is it really so crazy to believe that our minds can affect the conditions of our lives? They not only affect them but actually bring them into existence out of a sea of quantum possibilities. In a way that seems incomprehensible, but which is provable in the laboratory, we literally create the world we see with our awareness.

In addition to listening in meditation, I talked to God by praying in the manner of Religious Scientists, meaning that I tried to believe that the thing prayed for was already a fact. I began to "treat" my own aches and pains. My mood lifted and my worldview began to shift. I found myself thinking in terms of future achievements rather than dwelling on past disappointments.

This image of God as consciousness was something that *finally* comported with my broom closet vision. It was an intelligence permeating all things, the source and substance of the visible world, a loving presence that supports all life rather than standing in opposition to it, judging and censuring.

I began to entertain the idea that maybe—just *maybe*— life was good.

And so was God.

According to New Thought, "Whatever man can conceive and believe, man can achieve." It's not only our nature to create, it's our whole purpose in being here. My life was not to be endured, it was to be designed. My fate was not set but could be directed by my conscious mind and brought to fulfillment through unconscious processes. Rather than being alone, I was connected to all other things in the universe and everyone in it. As a part of creation, I was also a participant in its unfolding.

In short, *I mattered.* There was nothing opposing me, everything supporting me. Whatever I decided to do, as long as it "robbed no one and created no delusion," I was assured that universal consciousness had my back.

One Wednesday evening I splurged on a fifteen dollar class of Dr. Walker's. He handed us a blank piece of lined paper, asking us to list the things that we wanted out of life in order of their importance. Call me a monomaniac but I wrote only two words on the very first line:

Writing career.

Tip: "Pray without ceasing."

(1 Thessalonians 5:17)

Why? *Because you are, anyway.*

What is in your mind is the cause of your experience. When you think, it's like placing an online order for an item that will promptly be delivered.

Your thoughts are setting up an unconscious expectation, whether that's for something new and wonderful or for *more of the same*.

This is the essence of the Law of Attraction. *You* are cause; your life is the *effect.*

"Praying aright" means understanding that your thought is creative—of feelings, of the quality of your relationships, of physical things like health, prosperity, and the external circumstances of your life.

In other words, don't obsess on the things you don't like in your life. Forget them. Create something new by *thinking* something new, with the faith that your thought will bring about positive change.

Remember, all thought is a form of prayer.

End Tip

Experiment: Make friends and influence people.

Try this fun game. If there's someone at home or at work that's annoying you, do your best to release the anger and annoyance, if only for an hour or a day. Instead, force yourself to think respectful, loving thoughts about that person.

Then step back and watch the turnaround in his behavior. If you can pull this off, you'll see it work every time!

Caution: The douchebag may end up asking you out to lunch.

End Experiment

8

Have Yourself a Dominatrix Christmas

Shortly after I began to "listen to God," I had a call from a friend named John. We weren't close buddies, more like professional acquaintances. Now, after writing nearly a dozen scripts for three cable series he's produced, I consider him a friend—but at the time, a casual phone call was unexpected.

We first met when he directed and produced a children's film I brought into LIVE. He'd changed genres, as it turned out, having landed a deal at the Playboy Channel to produce some high-end erotica.

Dying for the chance to do something besides temping, I begged him for a job as a writer's assistant on the show.

"Why wouldn't you want to be a writer?" he asked.

"Oh yeah," I replied casually. "That's what I *meant* to say."

Finally, the chance to write a produced script. I pitched John a few ideas, two of which he liked. One was a rip-off (I mean *tribute to*) Dickens' *A Christmas Carol*. The other involved a country and western singer suffering from burnout.

The shows were shot at a mansion in the hills of Malibu, a peach-colored compound with a crystal blue swimming pool in a beautiful, rustic setting. The acting left something to be desired—but someone had *finally* paid me to write something besides a term paper!

Though it wasn't exactly what I'd had in mind all these years, at least it showed I wasn't completely deluded about my abilities. I was really looking forward to this new way of supplementing my income. It was fun and exciting.

However, John ended up getting some grief from Playboy about my shows. The Christmas one featured a dominatrix Ghost of Christmas Past who had to be flown into a bedroom window on wires, making it the most expensive episode of the series. Expense wasn't the main problem, though. It was the humor. John summed up Playboy's objections this way:

"Men don't think sex is funny."

Maybe not, but watching porn stars trying to act between sex scenes *is* hysterical, so you might as well run with it.

My foray into erotica at a standstill, I temped at the property management company in downtown LA, answering calls from bank branches with emergencies like clogged toilets and ant infestations. The very first day I got a call from a bank manager complaining of a bad smell in her supply closet. I didn't know whether to call the pest control folks to search for a dead rodent, the police to look for a corpse, or to recommend that the manager buy a carton of Tums for the break room. I don't remember what I did—probably put her on hold and forgot about her.

I soon learned the ropes and ended up staying there for months. It was great to be receiving a regular paycheck again, and the people I worked with were nice and normal, especially compared to those in the entertainment business. It was almost relaxing to go to work.

While employed there, I got a call from a director at Playboy who'd read my script *Natural Enemies*. It was a *film noir* set in Texas that had caught the interest of several producers before him. Paramount Home Video was going to produce it with Neo Films at one point, but the deal ended up falling through.

This guy loved the script and thought he could get it set up as a movie. Even though I was enjoying the relative sanity of the property management business, I still hankered to be a produced screenwriter. Sitting by the phone, I would will it to ring with news of my script's being optioned.

Instead, it rang with a bank manager wondering what to do about the cloud of red ink floating in his lobby. Turns out a dye-pack had exploded during an attempted robbery.

"Open a window!" says I, helpfully.

"There are no windows in banks."

"Oh."

(I hadn't learned *all* the ropes.)

This period was rich with irony: It had been twenty years since I'd graduated college, when the only work I could get was as a temp…*in a property management company*.

Don't misunderstand. I was not complaining. I was grateful for the job and for the reasonable people I worked with. Grateful, too, that I had decent, if outmoded, clothes hanging in my closet, and an old but semi-reliable car to get me to work. To look at me, you wouldn't know how desperate I'd been only months before.

Reporting to work in the downtown high-rise, I tried to mimic the carriage of the successful professionals I passed on my way in and out of the lobby. To earn overtime, I volunteered for nights and weekends, feeling a forgotten sense of workplace camaraderie as I signed in with the guard.

"Evening."

"Evening."

"They working ya hard?"

"They sure are."

I couldn't believe anyone wanted to "work me" at all. Slowly, I began to feel valued and worthy again. The confidence I'd at first only pretended to have was worming its way into my soul. Yes, I was back in the saddle…

but hardly creatively fulfilled.

Still, I'd been paid to write two TV scripts, and there had been new interest in *Natural Enemies*. Perhaps these were indicators of where I was headed.

I decided to keep the faith and keep praying.

Tip: "Watch for the signs."

New Thought minister Joseph R. Murphy said, "The subconscious will not take the trouble to work for those who don't believe in it."

Imagine that you were knocking yourself out for someone, doing everything you could to help them, but they continually ignored your efforts. You'd soon come to the conclusion that they didn't appreciate what they were doing, or even preferred that you stop altogether.

Watch for the signs, those small indicators that what you want is being delivered to you. Acknowledge them and say *Thank you*.

End Tip

9

Why I Believe Weird Things

I'm sorry to interrupt the flow of the narrative, but I need to acknowledge that from here on in things will get a little weird. It's no use denying that metaphysics involves a whole new way of looking at the world; in particular, a whole new way of thinking about *causation*.

Here's the gist:

Contrary to what most people believe, metaphysicians maintain that *we ourselves* are the cause of all of our experience, rather than any outside forces. Things don't happen to us, they happen *through* us.

Whatever happens in our lives is set up by our expectations, then is filtered through layers of education, social conditioning, and our own individual personalities, all of which tend to confirm those expectations:

They always told me that this is the way things were, and sure enough they were right!

Who you are and how you've been educated will determine the flavor of your experiences, as well as how satisfied you are with the taste.

Instead of Forrest Gump's box of chocolates, let's say life is like ice cream.

Did you have a vanilla upbringing? You'll likely be creating vanilla experiences throughout your entire life. Maybe your childhood was more like strawberry cream. That's how it will be for you.

But what if you want *Chunky Monkey* for a change? You've been dying to try it, but don't think you're entitled to it? It sounds so exotic, so out of your reach—

You will have to be able to imagine it before you can bring it into your experience, and that's tough to do when you've been raised with only one flavor.

Imagine this: You're standing over an infinite array of tubs, holding fresh yummy ice cream in every color: green, pink, yellow, purple, and every conceivable flavor: coffee, raspberry, chocolate swirl, lemon ice, marshmallow crunch. *Whatever you can imagine is there.* If you want to taste something different, you'll have to stop limiting yourself to the ice cream you already know, and start believing in that vast array of possibilities, just waiting for you to dunk your scoop into one or all of them.

If it's *Chunky Monkey* you want, and you imagine it with all your heart, some-*how* in some *way* it will appear, just as you desired. You'll be led to it, or someone will drop in for a visit carrying a tub, or maybe you'll get a coupon for it in the mail. Rest assured, if you come right out and ask for what you want, it's on its way to you.

Is there a catch?

Well, sure. There's always a catch. (They told you that, didn't they?)

All you have to do in order to make it work is to change your thinking about the nature of reality itself.

Admittedly that's a tall order. This is why most people don't experience the instant wish-granting genie thing. For manifestation techniques to work, you usually have to experience the gradual erosion of one belief system through the willingness to entertain new ideas, then witness "demonstrations" or "proofs" that follow this opening of the mind until enough of them accrue to convince you.

In other words, you *will* see proof of this if you can relax your tight grip on reality. Once you do, you'll be tasting all kinds of flavors, even those you didn't know existed.

You're going to *create* your own ice cream store.

A quick self-examination will reveal that your mouth is watering right now because of the ice cream analogy. (Unless you're lactose intolerant, in which case your stomach is rumbling. *Sorry*.) This is an essential part of the whole process, *feeling* what it is you want to experience.

The Universe will then match your feeling with experiences.

You may not even be reading anymore, having tossed aside the book, jumped into your car, and high-tailed it to the nearest Baskin & Robbins. See how that works? Our imaginations *compel* us.

Our imaginations also compel the outer reality to conform to *them*.

Many people think I'm bat-shit crazy for making these assertions. Among them is my cousin, a very practical and reasonable woman who once suggested I might enjoy a book called *Why People Believe Weird Things* by Michael Shermer.

One reason I'm writing this is so that when my friends and loved ones[*] want to know why I think the way I do, I can hand them a copy of my book and go about my business. Imagine trying to encapsulate all of your experience, all of your research, and all of your thought processes into a casual conversation about *everything,* including life and death and the nature of existence, over a turkey leg at Thanksgiving. Now throw in a God sighting, some psychic experiences, and a miracle or two, and you've got yourself a sound reputation as the family flake.

More explanation is required. If you dole out tidbits in the "strangest thing happened" vein, it can be maddening to others. With no frame of reference, they can think you're messing with them, or confabulating to make yourself more interesting, or that you were simply blessed with a "vivid imagination."

---

[*] That's not a sop. I really do love them.

God forbid you should claim to have received a blessing as the result of prayer. They will check your forehead for fever, tactfully inquiring as to whether you're experiencing double vision.

You don't need to be religious, spiritual, or even very open-minded to know that the world is not always as it appears. Every day we find weirdness mixed in with our ordinary experience. In the past, religion filled in the gaps nicely, making God the catch-all for anything that wasn't readily understood.

It's a miracle, case closed. Now, shut up and drink your communion wine.

These days, scientists are doing a yeoman's job of explaining the physical universe, but when it comes to the miraculous they look—or even run—the other way. They seem to think that anything that is not repeatable in a controlled, double-blind laboratory experiment, or that doesn't operate according to accepted principles, can't have happened in the first place so there's no point in trying to explain it. It's the very definition of a closed system, like a little boy's treehouse with the words **No Miracullz Allowed** posted over the door.

Traditional science is very useful when the world is behaving itself: The sun rises, the sun sets. Rain falls and the earth gets wet. Rain freezes and snow blankets the ground. Metals are heavy and gases are light. We can't walk through walls and we don't know what others are thinking, and we certainly can't know what will happen in a future that has yet to occur.

Yes, everything in our world makes beautiful sense…

Until it doesn't.

For every accepted law, rule, or fact, there is an exception. Every single one. I am not making this up. Any honest scientist will tell you the same. The famous mystic Sri Aurobindo once observed that the physical laws of the universe aren't actually fixed laws but more like *suggestions.*

Although chemistry is supposed to be one of the hard sciences, in his book *Seven Experiments that Could Change the World* biologist Rupert Sheldrake demonstrates that expectation plays a part even in chemical reactions. When told they should arrive at a result *other* than the one universally found in the textbooks, beginning chemistry students got the result they were instructed to get, rather than the "right" one.

This proves conclusively that our expectations affect the outer world. In other words:

Expectation (belief, imagination) trumps "reality."

Why haven't you heard of Sheldrake's ground-breaking experiment?

Beats me.

My suspicion is that too many people are invested in this world just the way it is, and I suppose they have a point. How could we function in a shifting Dali-esque landscape of melting buildings and disappearing objects? It wouldn't be very manageable. But don't worry, the world as you know it is not going anywhere. It's as solid and as real as it appears to be— *around ninety-nine percent of the time.*

However, if you don't happen to like your own personal landscape, for example your own level of health, you can change it if you first understand that it is permeable, flexible, and changeable, and very susceptible to the working of your imagination.

Then there's the issue of "spontaneous remission." This is what it's called when a disease simply disappears for no apparent reason. When confronted with such a medical miracle, the doctor labels it with this official-sounding phrase and closes the file. *Why* something healed immediately or overnight cannot be determined, so it's dealt with in a way that allows the doc to walk away with his dignity intact. It could just as easily be labeled "Hell if I know!" but that would tend to undermine the doctor's authority.

The placebo effect (or placebo response) presents an even bigger quandary:

If you're given an inert sugar pill that is presented as medication, it has a thirty percent chance of being effective. That means that virtually *one third* of the time, the "Hell if I know!" theory of medicine is in play. [*]

How do you teach that in medical school?

I've recently heard about a thing called honest placebos. This involves revealing to the patient ahead of time that the

---

[*] New information: It's now thought to be as high as 66%.

syringe he's about to be injected with contains a harmless substance like salt water. What do you think happens when the sensible, intelligent patient is told he's being administered something with no power whatsoever to heal him?

He *still* receives a healing benefit from the shot!

How is this different from the fundamentalist preacher who smacks the congregant on the forehead, telling him to heal in the name of *the Lord Jeeeezus*...? It's clearly a matter of a subconscious conditioning to accept healing from one source or the other: Christ or the man in the lab coat.

Imagine what would happen if, instead of being encouraged to "Ask your doctor if you're healthy enough for sexual activity," there were commercials urging you to "Go ask your doctor for a Big-Ass Miracle!"

The line between science and spirituality is becoming ever more blurred. It's not simply a question of mind over matter, but whether there was ever any "matter" to begin with. It appears that there isn't—at least, not in the way we're used to thinking of it. There are no "things," only differing levels of mind and energy.

Physicist John A. Wheeler put it this way: "There's no *out there* out there."

I find it more interesting to explore the exceptions to the rules rather than bowing to the rules themselves. I like it when things don't go according to plan, because miracles emerge from cracks in the established order.

Here's the funny thing about miracles:

If you've signed up for a version of reality in which they can't and don't occur, where they represent some kind of cosmic bad manners, they probably won't happen. They will honor you and your belief system by not crashing your party. They're very considerate that way.

However, if you want...

BIG-ASS MIRACLES,

you have to make room for them in your experience. Until you open your heart and welcome them, they will shy away like rubber moles ducking your mental mallet.

But once they peek out and see that it's safe, the little buggers will pop up all over the place!

That's a promise.

Tip: Try to be less rational.

I'm serious.

You have been lied to—unintentionally, surely—about the nature of existence and your part in it.

You are not only part of creation, you are one of its *creators*. You can't be on this Earth without creating. It's not possible. Everything you think, everything you do and say, constitutes an act of creation. It's simply the nature of things.

To become a *deliberate* creator, you must first accept the above idea, then look at all of your beliefs pertaining to matters scientific, legal, religious, political, historical, societal, and anything I've left out—understanding that they, too, are creations; that is to say, *something someone made up*. Once made up and reinforced through textbooks, religious rituals, laws, "common wisdom," experimentation, myths and stories, and any of *those* I've left out, things tend to stick—both in our awareness, as well as in "reality."

Our reality didn't arrive here whole; it was *built*. And it's still under construction, which is why you may hit a few traffic jams as you travel down the road of life.

Physicist John Wheeler also said, "It's a participatory universe."

You participate, knowingly or otherwise. If you're here, you can't help having an effect. You're either reinforcing the world as you found it or willfully changing it, both in terms of your personal experience *and* of the larger picture.

Whew. That's a lot of responsibility.

Yet as soon as you begin to question everything you once took for granted, you are on your way to creating remarkable experiences in your life. You can make up something totally new and wonderful!

And when the rational part of your mind starts to argue with this proposition, ask it to consider the following:

The universe itself is not rational, reasonable, or logical.

What's rational about a giraffe? How many reasonable babies have you met? Where's the logic in a rose?

We take such pride in our capacity for reasoning. It is a *tool*—one among many useful tools for dealing with life—but it doesn't define us any more than it does a giraffe or a baby or a rose.

Try to see the world through the lens of wonder rather than through the lens of materialism, and it will reveal more and more of its wonders to you. When you stop believing that you or anyone else has all the answers, very strange and wonderful things can occur.

Those things are new acts of creation.

End Tip

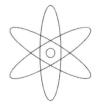 **Experiment: Do the Chunky Monkey!**

Take a flier on this little experiment.

If it suits your taste buds, tell the Universe you'd like some Chunky Monkey ice cream. (No, I'm not a spokesperson for Ben & Jerry's, I just like the name.)

Think about it day and night, imagining the tastes, temperature, and textures: delicious chewy chocolate fudge on a bed of banana cream with rich walnut chunks. *Mmmm.* When people want to know why you're smacking your lips and drooling onto your paperwork all day, just tell them you're on a new medication or something.

Do this until the ice cream or something similar, like a banana split, shows up in your life from some unexpected source. At the very least, you should see a pop-up ad for it on your computer screen.

Ernest Holmes called this a "demonstration." When you can prove to yourself that small prayers are answered, you just might start believing it will work with the big stuff too.

Be sure to drop me a note at the Big-Ass Miracle Café forum when this happens, and in the meantime, *bon appétit, mes petits singes!*

End Experiment

10

The Dream Cottage

*A*fter a long separation Rajeev and I decided to give it another try; we'd been getting along much better since I'd discovered Religious Science. He even came to church with me a few times, braving the show tunes to see what I found so interesting. Imagine my surprise when he told me this idea of "manifesting with thought" was central to Hinduism, as well.

Now you tell me about Hinduism?

We started to look for an apartment together. I was temping at the property management company, he was working at a small film distributor. Finding a new place with no money in the bank was going to be a challenge. That was especially true for Santa Monica, which is one of the most desirable places to live because it's close to the beach and has cleaner air and cooler temperatures as a result. You could still find rent-controlled apartments, which meant there was fierce competition for even the cheesiest, boxiest places—those with spray-on ceilings, no parking, and echoing courtyards. We spent every weekend for a month and a half going from apartment to apartment with no results.

Finally I told Rajeev that I couldn't do it anymore. He asked what I proposed doing instead. I told him I'd use Religious Science to get us a new place, my first time putting the new philosophy to a practical test. I could see he was dubious but didn't let that faze me. Mama was sick of house-hunting.

Sitting on my bed (hereinafter known as "The Magic Bed") I went into meditation, visualizing the space I wanted. My desired list of features was absurd given our financial situation: a hardwood floor, arched doorways, a garden plot, plenty of parking, a walking neighborhood... and charming, it had to be charming.

After I'd done this visualization exercise or "treatment" for several days, Rajeev showed me a newspaper ad for a rent-controlled house in Santa Monica. I must have contracted amnesia about my own prayers because I said he could forget about calling. Santa Monica landlords had their choice of tenants, I assured him, and they wouldn't want *us*.

He called anyway. Hearing his name, the landlord said in a thick Persian accent, "You are Indian? I like the Indian people."

He invited us to look at the house, a white wooden cottage with a red gabled roof on a tree-lined street. Rajeev went by to get the key, and while he was doing something else, I went to see it myself during a rainstorm. The electricity was off so I had to use a flashlight to view the interior, laughing out loud when the beam caught the bungalow's arched doorways, genuine hardwood floors, fireplace with a carved mantelpiece, and mullioned casement windows. There were windows everywhere, a whole wall of them in the second room that would make a perfect office. I didn't see the rose bush and the Bird of Paradise until after we'd moved in.

Rajeev called me later to see if I liked it. All I could say was, "It's exactly right."

We met with the landlord to fill out the forms. He showed us a folder containing a stack of applications an inch thick, and told us he'd decided to pass up all those other applicants and let us have the house *just like that*.

Sheepishly, I informed him that I'd declared bankruptcy the year before. He dismissed my concern with a shrug. I promptly wrote him a bad check for the deposit, which he didn't try to cash until there were funds in the account. Best of all, when we moved them in our two cats seemed right at home.

I don't know about you but the whole thing struck *me* as a miracle. (It still does.)

Once our accommodations were taken care of, I set out to improve my career.

Tip: Try to forget "common wisdom."

In this case, I'm not referring to formal education, but to the knowledge you have of the world, your certainty of how people will react to what it is you want to do, with this or that inevitable result.

You tell the world how it's going to be with you, not the other way around. I don't care what you look like, what you weigh, what your race is—*it's of little importance.* Your mindset, your habits of thought, your beliefs, consciously or unconsciously held, are what determine your experience at absolutely every step of the way.

Don't let "them" tell you how to think!

End Tip

Experiment: Learn to meditate and do it daily.

It's not at all mysterious. You just zone out, trying to forget your daily concerns, resulting in a kind of half-sleep or state of self-hypnosis. A good start would be to take ten or twenty minutes of quiet, uninterrupted time (cell phone off) when you simply concentrate on your breathing, letting your mind drift.

Meditation causes your brain waves to synchronize, leading to a more focused and more intelligent you. It also lowers your heart rate and blood pressure by calming your parasympathetic nervous system, leading to a more stable and healthier you.

This part of it, however, *is* mysterious: When you have more practice, you can start seeding your unconscious mind with your desires in this receptive, loosey-goosey state of mind. If you meditate on a thing with the intention of causing it to happen, it tends to manifest in the outer world.

End Experiment

11

I "Treat" Myself to a Writing Job at Dimension Films

*R*emember Neo Films? They were the guys who had tried to produce my original scripts years before.

They had changed their name to Neo Art & Logic, and had done very well in the interim. Among many other films, they made the priceless documentary *Trekkies*, which was acquired by Paramount, and the supernatural thriller *Prophecy*, financed by the low-budget division of Miramax, Dimension Films. Headed up by Harvey Weinstein's brother Bob, Dimension was busy buying up all of the horror franchises of the seventies and eighties. Neo became a virtual in-house production arm for the sequels.

I had remained friends with one of the partners, and while we were out for a catch-up dinner, he surprised me by offering me a job in development. The salary was low and it would only last for six months—I would be paid from the production budget of *Mimic II*—but it would be an opportunity to get back into showbiz. A risk to be sure—but if not then, when?

Meanwhile, the property management company offered me a fulltime position with a nice salary and benefits. With Rajeev's blessing, and some regret, I turned down the better paying job and went to work reading scripts for Neo.

I solicited, read, and evaluated a hundred screenplays. A few of them were good enough to run past by the partners, but nothing caught their interest. Though I was glad to be in a creative atmosphere, I was frustrated by all of the mediocre writing I had to read. Many times I wanted to shout, *Over here! Got your great screenwriter right here! Give me a whirl!*

I began working at Neo in September of 1999. In October, I wrote this in my journal:

Ltg 10-04-99

I think I know now what they mean in Sci of Mind (sic) when they talk of not compromising, because I just said the most uncompromising prayer ever.

It went like this:

I reject working at Neo. I reject working as a temp. I reject working in property management. I reject working as an assistant to anyone. I reject every other method of making a living other than as a writer.

One day when my producer friend returned from Canada, he took me out to lunch. (A lot of low-budget production is done in Canada because the Canadian government subsidizes films the way we do farms.) I told him that one of the other guys had asked me to flesh out an idea he had for a ghost story, and he replied, "If you want to write something, why don't you do a treatment for Children of the Corn VII? We have to produce it and there's no script."

Based on a Stephen King short story, the original *Children of the Corn* is now considered a horror classic. It centers around a group kids in the Heartland who become possessed by an evil spirit haunting the cornfields, and who start to kill the townspeople in atonement for their sins. (Or something.)

My story idea involved a long-ago tent revival that had gone up in flames. The children who died in the conflagration returned decades later to torment an elderly survivor.

The guys at Neo loved it, but that was only the first step. The treatment would have to be approved by Dimension, who had sent out a call for ideas to a bunch of writers, most of whom were young males. I was a woman with no credits and no agent, having reached the age at which you're officially supposed to be embalmed in the entertainment industry—a business which, more than any other with the possible exception of the NFL, is still dominated by men. I tried to maintain my cool, but didn't do so well with that, as can be seen here:

Ltg 01-06-00

The high that I was on after realizing that they were going to submit my treatment is almost completely gone. Feeling pessimistic, might as well say it. How can I not be, after hearing that A Band Apart is also submitting a treatment?

And once I realize that I am becoming pessimistic, I need to change my thinking.

I fought back the pessimism by affirming over and over that I would get the job. Meditating on The Magic Bed, I imagined it as a done deal. After a few weeks of this, there was a meeting with a local Miramax executive named Steve, who told me that the writing sample I'd submitted (*Natural Enemies*) had been evaluated and determined to be a "no" for production but a "consider" for the writer. Steve liked my *Corn* idea but said his New York counterpart, who was Bob Weinstein's assistant and a budding production executive himself, was not in favor of it. Steve assured me he'd get it past him, though, and when the meeting was over he shook my hand and said he looked forward to working with me.

It was time to leave for the day. I got in my car and drove west on Santa Monica Boulevard. Before reaching the freeway, I had to pull over, feeling sick at my stomach. Leaning on the steering to do some deep breathing, I kept hearing David Walker's words in my head:

"This stuff works. It really, really works."

I don't think I'd really believed it until that moment. The Dream Cottage *could* have been a fluke, an unusual piece of good luck. It had been a year since I'd attended that class in which I'd written the words "writing career." In between, I'd temped and had almost accepted a fulltime job in property management, but couldn't let go of the dream.

Could prayer have been the missing ingredient during all those years of struggle? It was beginning to look that way. Still, I was afraid of getting ahead of myself, having endured so many reversals of fortune in the past. Here's what I wrote in my journal after the meeting with Steve:

Ltg 01-28-00

The meeting yesterday was amazing. Steve said they had read five treatments and decided to go with this one.

They've read twenty or thirty sample scripts, and I think the implication was that Natural Enemies was good. Anyway, he said he had total confidence that I could deliver the script.

There followed some back and forth about the deal. Still deathly afraid it would fall through, I went into meditation one day and heard the words, "The deal is closed; the gift is made." Writing that down in my journal, I tried to get a stranglehold on the belief that this was all coming to me through affirmative prayer.

It was taking forever for Miramax to commit. The development job was coming to an end, and I'd soon need paying work again. My arm was stretched out so far trying to grasp the brass ring that I was about to fall off of the horse. The money was running out, my husband was urging me to get a job, and there was turmoil at the production company over some other project.

But then I got the call(s):

Ltg 04-12-00 D-Day

Went to get my messages and there were five! Freak-out, panic, heart attack.

Two from Keith in Toronto, one from Lauren, two from Louis.

> Louis: Bob was very impressed. I want you to start writing (gave me some notes), said he's not the money guy, but they'll work something out.

Within a week, I'd written the script, submitting it to the Neo gang to get their notes before emailing it to New York. Meanwhile, Miramax was talking about giving me an overall deal.

Ltg 04-25-00

> From temping to submitting a treatment to Miramax Films in one year. No, from being employed as a secretary to having a WRITING DEAL with Miramax Films in one year.
>
> Lauren called with Joel on conference, and he said I'd done the impossible: Everyone there likes the script! He said it's a first.
>
> I AM a working writer.

Dimension loved my draft, and I was indeed offered the long-term deal. One of the junior execs declared I would be their "go-to" girl for the low-budget horror flicks. I hired a lawyer to negotiate the contract, which laid out the step-by-step, draft-by-draft fees on upwards of ten films. My producer friend advised against doing that deal because it would lock me into lower fees, but my eyes were already bugging at the dollar amounts in the contract. I'd lived very close to the bone for years, and they were offering me a potential fortune.

There was no guarantee it was going to continue, however. I'd learned that things can change very quickly at Miramax, having seen one of their new favorites lose favor overnight.

Could I count on this?

I'd promised myself long ago that if I ever got my hands on a sum larger than a few hundred dollars, I'd bank it and go back to work at whatever job I could get to keep the money flowing. Never again would I go broke trying to launch some kind of artistic project.

In this entry, I'd been mulling that prospect with Rajeev:

Ltg 05-08-00

I told him about a "crisis of faith." To wit, do I sock the money away and find another means of making expense money, or do I use the script money to support me in further writing and spiritual pursuits?

He shocked me by saying exactly what I wanted to hear!

But later that month the deal still was not done:

Ltg 05-29-00

Must get my shit together.

Have been treating like crazy, but am suffering from more or less acute anxiety. As I said to Rajeev, if there's any sacrilege in this religion, that's it.

Got a little testy with God this morning. Don't feel like writing. Don't feel like being grateful.

May be tied to the fact that I don't have my deal yet and the money's running out. May be tied to insecurity over the quality of the script or God knows what, but I feel like the old me, the nervous me, the avoid what you need to do me.

And I like it not one bit.

I didn't hear from them, and the longer I didn't hear, the more doubtful I became. Was it true that this stuff really, really worked?

Ltg 06-19-00

Had a call from Keith. I said they've had the script for a week and I haven't heard. He says that's typical. He wouldn't panic at all, it's a really good script.

Finally the universe delivered:

Ltg 6-21-00

Glad I got out of bed for that call. It was Dan at Irwin's office saying the check is here. Hallelujah!

I scored fifteen thousand dollars for that script, plus rewrites. The film was of course shot in Canada, and the producers ended up hating most of the actors' performances so they cut the film down to the barest possible storyline, which consisted of a scantily clad female skulking down the hallways of a condemned apartment building, freaked out of her wits by some creepy kids and eerie sound effects.

And of course, the Killer Corn.

The main villain of the King story was a spiritual entity the children referred to as "He who walks between the rows." During our story meetings, we'd shorten that to "Hewho," as in—

"So, Hewho turns the kids into zombies and they go around killing the residents of the apartment building? How do we kill the stripper in the bathtub? Is that Hewho, too?" It goes without saying that you must have a stripper in a cheap horror film, someone who will shed her clothes no matter what else is going on in the scene, right? These movies are made with fourteen-year-old boys in mind. (Also forty-year-old boys.)

It was one of the Neo guys, Joel, who suggested the Killer Corn Kernels. A zombie kid throws them into the tub with the aforementioned stripper, whereupon giant tendrils spring out of the water, strangling her like vegetal boas.

Doing the movie was a blast. Sadly, it wasn't nominated for an Academy Award. Recently it was shown on cable with a rating of half a star.

Most of the process had been out of my control. There were all of the executives to accommodate with their notes, and then there was the acting, which wasn't much better than that in the Playboy shows. Nevertheless, I was pretty much over the moon with it all. I had been paid to write a feature film, only a year and a half after I'd declared bankruptcy. Not only that, I had an overall deal with a mini-major.

Verily, I say unto thee—it was frigging amazing. And it *had* to be due to my new way of thinking.

By this time I'd begun using mind games to help me write. The process of getting an approved outline had been long and difficult. The first one had taken six months! I was giddy when it was finally green-lighted, but the joy of being hired was soon replaced with the dread of having to write the script.

Here's what I did: I told myself that the script was already written. I knew I was going to get it done somehow, which meant it was sitting out there in a completed form in the future, waiting for me to reach out and grab it. All I had to do was to move my fingers across the keyboard, striking the keys that corresponded to the words that had already been written. *Easy*!

This game actually helps to take the pressure off. You convince yourself you're not *writing*, but only transcribing. And who's to say you're *not* downloading something from the Big

Hologram in the sky that contains all human experience, past, present and future—what the mystics refer to as *The Akashic Records*? It's supposedly the library documenting everything that happens on earth, past, present, future—and everything created, whether it's Dostoyevsky or Dr. Seuss. If you need a schlocky horror script, you merely swipe your card and then download it to your computer.

If that's true, why aren't you a literary genius? Why just a hack?

Rather than worrying about what's "true" ask yourself—*Is it a useful idea?* If it is, then use it.

And you know what? I like being a hack. It suits my temperament and talents. I've found my water level and I'm sticking to it. Remember, Ernest Holmes said that all things are possible with treatment as long as "they rob no one and create no delusion." I'm not thieving, and unless I delude myself into thinking my writing is for the ages instead of pure entertainment, we have no problem. I may not be Lillian Hellman but these days I don't mind being me.

In utilizing this science you start with the raw material you were born with and go from there. I once told a friend about the things he could do with R.S. and he popped out with, "So I can get a supermodel to date me?" (I *think* he was kind of serious.)

What could I say except, "You might want to acquire the jet and the private island *before* you go after the international beauties." He seemed to think he could *blink* a babe into existence, with nothing to interest the girl when she got there. This isn't about having outlandish fantasies, it's about really making things happen. If he'd wanted an attractive mate who was well suited to him, he could have had one easily.[*]

Even though I was thrilled to be writing professionally, things were not entirely peachy. After a very short time the New York executive began driving me insane. Once I'd been given the assignment he'd call every three hours expecting to see something. He was always calling, calling, calling while I was trying to write.

"Bob needs to see pages!" he'd shriek in my ear.

"Well, I have to write them first, and I can't write them when I'm on the phone with you!"

His notes were on the order of: "You don't have a dead body until page ten. Gimme a bloody corpse on page two." Or: "The lead actress has to take her shirt off in the first act!" Harkening back to my days at Playboy, he told me to "get the cutesy stuff" out of the script, which I took to mean "the wit."

After The Corn Kids, my next assignment was to write a draft of a sequel to *The Faculty*. What I hadn't counted on was exactly *how* low-budget these films were. In effect they told me: "There's no money for sets, actors, or special effects...*go!*" I had to imagine a scenario that could be horrifying with no mood

---

[*] I'm going to retract that, and say that he *could* conjure up a supermodel if he was willing to do the work in consciousness. However, it might take a *lot* of work, and I'm betting that someone who achieves that level of mind has more important things on his plate than hustling hot babes.

enhancements other than fake blood, thick make-up, and low lighting. I wrote a good script, anyway. As far as I know it was never produced.

Around this time Bob Weinstein came to town for meetings with his west coast people. He requested one with me, which made the frantic NY executive even more frantic. Bob apparently liked my work, and this guy hadn't wanted to hire me in the first place. He was terrified I'd say something bad about him to Bob. I know this because he said, "You're not going to say anything bad about me to Bob, are you?"

Arriving at the Miramax building, I was so nervous I bumped my head getting out of the car. The valet guys got a good laugh out of this. Now both humiliated *and* anxious, I took the elevator to the floor where the meeting was scheduled, only to be told it was postponed until two hours later. I went back down to the parking garage and drove all of the way home to eat lunch.

It was a humid day. I was perspiring heavily and my hair had gone frizzy. When the time finally arrived for the meeting, the junior exec came out to greet me in the waiting room. He was so short he barely reached the bottom of my chin, making me feel like a big sweaty Yeti as I was escorted into the conference room. There I met Bob and his team, who were seated around a large table. The executives had the disconcerting habit of furiously scribbling notes every time Bob opened his mouth.

I tried to do the same, but he waved me off, saying the guys would keep track of the conversation. "How did we find you?" Bob wanted to know.

Taken aback by the question, I began babbling something about having been an executive myself once upon a time. He soon cut me off, saying he had a plum assignment for me—re-envisioning the Halloween franchise, now on its twentieth outing. He warned me that the rights owner had submitted his own script, but maintained that no one at Miramax liked it. They wanted something new. Perhaps I'd like to meet with the gentleman to pitch him something?

The frantic exec was shaking his head in my peripheral vision. Bob took whatever hint that was and dismissed me from the meeting. He said they'd call me to hear my ideas and gave me a copy of the existing script to read.

Working on an anniversary edition of Halloween was an exciting prospect. This was one feature that would be released theatrically instead of going straight to video, and was set to star the original heroine, Jamie Lee Curtis. Who didn't love Jamie Lee Curtis?

I had to come up with a new take on the film in only a couple of days. As soon as they returned to New York they'd be calling to hear what I had.

After reading their script, I laid down to ponder it on The Magic Bed. Staring at the ceiling, I asked for something to come to me. Soon a story began to unfold, a visual and auditory experience that was so complete it was like watching a finished movie. The whole process took about two hours.

I hopped up from the bed and wrote it all down. Then I waited, quaking, for my phone call.

There's this thing I do when I get nervous: My voice seizes up. If it comes out at all, it's as querulous an old lady's. The inability to control it has been my albatross for years. Though I've sought help for it, nothing's ever worked. I endure it the best I can.

While anticipating the conference call from Bob Weinstein & Co., I received a pre-call from the pipsqueak exec. If you are the nervous type, you know that nothing makes you more nervous than someone drawing attention to your nervousness. So naturally, just before I was to be patched into the conference call with Bob and five other executives, he said, "Whatever you do, don't do that weird thing with your voice."

Accchhh!

I'd drunk two cups of chamomile tea, and I'd draped a blanket over myself while I sat in the kitchen so I wouldn't shiver from cold. (The Dream Cottage is drafty.) Still, when I heard all of those people introduced over the phone and knew that I'd be broadcasting from a speakerphone, my voice went wonky. Bob asked, "What's wrong with your voice, are you sick?"

"No, just weird," I replied, and then somehow launched into my pitch. As the positive reactions started coming in, I

83

relaxed and got into it. When it was done, they seemed really jazzed about the story. Later as I delivered pages, Bob was reported to have exulted, "This is a real movie!"

> Ltg 01-03-01
>
> Just got off the conference call with Bob. Got the job for Halloween. My re-write. Prayed for it; got it.
>
> Jesus H. Christ. What a difference a few prayers make. I will have no fewer than three feature credits this year. Corn, Faculty II and Halloween (I hope).[*]

Using the "transcribing" technique, I finished the script in a week, which left them dumbfounded. The same executives who had so intimidated me were now raving about the end product. One of them told me it was a first in the history of the company.

However, there was one story element that the frantic executive insisted would have to go. He said Bob would hate it. One of my characters was a Goth girl, a tattooed, very in-your-face person who cursed like a sailor and was completely indifferent to what people thought of her. When the character is cornered by the psychopathic Michael Myers, she doesn't cower, but juts out her chin and tells him to bring it.

We cut away from the action, assuming she's as dead as the other characters will soon be, but in the end when all of the

---

[*] Wrong. Although I was paid to work on those projects, I was only credited on *Corn*.

bodies have been arrayed in various states of gruesome death, we cut again to the highway and see the Goth chick walking backwards down the road, thumbing a ride, very much alive.

It was my favorite part of the script, a Thecla in the Lions' Den display of courage. When the girl stood up to him, the monster simply turned away. He had no appetite for someone who didn't fear death.

Too bad the character didn't make it to the screen. She would have been a welcome variation on the "virgin as victim" trope, as well as a kind of wish fulfillment for me. I would love to possess the kind of courage that caused all of my boogeymen to shrink away in confusion: money issues, authority figures, the IRS.

Dimension loved my draft, but the owner of the Halloween franchise was against it. He thought I'd given Michael supernatural powers by causing the house to shake in one scene. If you've read this far, you know that I don't really distinguish between natural and supernatural, but he felt it was out of character for the series.

At his insistence they went with the original script. I think I'll post the one I wrote on my website in case anyone wants to compare it with the finished film, which I never saw.

Although my screenplay wasn't used, I was now in solid with Dimension. Bob Weinstein himself called with my next assignment, which was to re-envision a script that had already been through several rewrites. The original idea belonged to

Kevin Williamson of *Scream* and *The Faculty* fame, a werewolf movie called *Cursed*.

"I don't want to see werewolves running all over Manhattan," Bob told me. I wasn't quite sure how to take that—a werewolf movie *sans* werewolves? I was starting to think I might have to pass on this one, but he insisted I meet with Kevin about it.

Kevin had written two iconic horror features and was the creator of *Dawson's Creek* and was also a close friend of Bob's. I was inching up to the big-time—not just direct-to-video fare, but a theatrical release with big-name talent. Once again thoroughly intimidated, I drove to his office on Sunset Boulevard to pitch him my ideas.

At least I didn't bang my head on anything this time. As it turned out, he put me at ease with his scathing sense of humor. I found that talking story with a creative person rather than a bunch of executives was much more enjoyable and had no problem spitting out my spiel.

Unfortunately, at the end of the meeting Kevin confirmed that my take was not what they had in mind. "But you'd be fun to work with," he said on parting.

Getting the assignment would have meant stepping out of my new comfort zone. So although I was sorry, at the same time I was relieved. I enjoyed being a go- to girl for cheap, below-the-radar movies. It meant steady work and decent money. If I stayed where I was, I'd be less likely to fail.

To my chagrin I got the job anyway, along with the supervision of the whole new crop of executives, no longer just the junior types. Now I was receiving calls from one senior executive in New York and another one in Los Angeles every few hours. I had no idea how to write a werewolf movie without werewolves. I felt the panic rising as I read the first twenty pages that had been written by Kevin. My job was to continue the story where he'd left off.

I did my bed magic, and a week later I had a first draft that featured only *a single* werewolf leaping across the Manhattan skyline. I was proud of it, but still dreaded turning it in. Somehow I knew it was going to bomb. I handed it to my lawyer and told him to submit it to the LA executive who'd been calling me, along with an invoice.

It was Kevin who called me next: "Why did you give the script to Miramax? Didn't you know I was the producer?"

"No," I told him. I had no idea what the chain of command was. All I knew was that I'd been under constant pressure by the executives to get them something immediately, and I had complied.

Kevin also wanted to know why I hadn't used all of the pages he'd written. *What?* Apparently, the executive had given me the wrong material to start with. I explained to Kevin that I'd used exactly what was given to me. He hung up, exasperated.

I never heard from him or Miramax again except through my lawyer, who informed me they'd offered to pay fifty cents on the dollar for the unwritten second draft. My meteoric rise had fizzled out in the heady atmosphere of the big-time. I'd gone out not with a bang, but a whimper.

The final script was ultimately written by someone else. I didn't see the finished product starring Christina Ricci, but I'm told there's only an occasional blurry shot of some fangs—no killer canines running around. The film was reportedly plagued with problems. Scenes had to be reshot using a stand-in for Christina, who'd long since moved on to another project.

Perhaps it was my time to move on, as well. The eight short months I'd worked for Dimension had nearly sent me around the bend. Needing to decompress, I spent some time gardening and rereading *The Science of Mind.*

What can I say? The new, philosophical me decided that the Miramax deal wasn't meant to be. Not long-term, anyway. I began to view the episode not so much as a failure, but as a lesson in being careful what you pray for. I'd been well paid as a writer-for-hire. They'd reportedly called me a "genius" for delivering good scripts so fast. Then somehow I had pissed off Bob or Kevin or both of them, and my tenure had come to an end.

But hold on there, Bucko!

Had it been the best use of whatever talent I had to be tacking endless sequels onto classic horror films, now reduced to the direct-to-video fare sitting on the shelves of the corner stores I used to haunt as a salesperson?

Hell no, it wasn't!

That's why the Miramax thing went away, so I could do something more personally meaningful. I hadn't wanted to be a writer so I could pump out cheesy horror scripts, I wanted to express myself. And I wanted to do it without someone cracking a whip over me.

Now, thanks to Bob & Co., I had the money to do just that. Finally, I understood the strange workings of Universal Consciousness, which had cleared the way for me to do what I'd been placed on this earth to do by getting my ass fired!

(However, I didn't get started right away...)

Tip: You haven't started your journal, yet?!

This is really important or I wouldn't rag on you about it. I mean, it really is kind of the whole point of the book.

You know, *this* one, that I've put my blood, sweat and tears into, spending countless backbreaking hours at the computer after waking at the crack of dawn and not stopping until the wee hours, my body going to flab, eyesight fading, head pounding with a caffeine headache and my complexion going pasty under these harsh fluorescent lights, while others are out playing tennis or romping at the beach or eating gourmet food instead of the nonfat cottage cheese I have been reduced to because there is no time to exercise while I'm here writing this book in order that **YOU** may lead a more fulfilling life...

Here's a gentle reminder of what you should do:

Write down what you want to happen in your life, then study it and memorize it as you would an important class assignment.

The printed word has authority. What the mind sees in print, it tends to accept.

As discussed earlier, you have your conscious mind, and you have your expanded mind. According to Dr. Bruce Lipton, author of *The Biology of Belief,* the conscious mind can process around 40 bits of information per second versus 40 *million* bits per second in the unconscious mind. The vast portion of your mental capacity is hunkering down and watching—seeing all, hearing all, absorbing and recording all, without your awareness of it. This part of your mind even has access to the future, as well as to the minds of others. *It* is not limited by time and space.

One thing you accomplish by journaling is telling your unconscious mind what it is that you want, while *bypassing* your Inner Naysayer, that smarty-pants conscious mind that can't even remember someone's *phone number* but still thinks it knows everything. And it just *knows* you can't have what you want.

Considering, as Dr. Lipton claims, that we are run by our unconscious 95% of the time, you can see the value of getting it on board with your plan. It knows all, has every resource at its disposal, and is running the show—but *without* its own agenda. It's following yours, as revealed through the things you think about, plan, and believe.

Tell it what you want. It will make it happen.

Your journal will also serve as a record, helping you put things in order when you're trying to remember how some miracle came about. Without it, timelines become fuzzy, the progression of events is difficult to track. But when it is right there in print— your description of what you wanted, written at a time when you had no reason to believe it would actually occur—and then it does happen, you have the proof that it was something both asked for and received.

This is a powerful tool for overcoming doubt. When things that you wrote about show up in your life, it leaves little room for the conscious mind to deny that there's a causal relationship between the two.

Of course, it will still try to explain things away by yelling, "Coincidence!" But over time, it will be less and less shrill until it sounds like a frustrated little mouse, squeaking off somewhere in a dark corner of your awareness.

End Tip

Experiment: Plagiarize your right brain.

God bless the left brain and its analytical capacity. If it weren't for it, we'd never be able to structure a story or organize a book.

However, when I want a great idea, it's the last place I turn. If you need fresh thinking, you have to allow the creative part of your mind to assist you. The right brain is just *full* of ideas; it has no limits because the imagination itself has no limits. Dreams are Righty's stock in trade.

Let's say you have a problem with a book, a story, a song, or any creative endeavor. Simply write down a description of the problem before you go to sleep, along with a request for your sleeping mind to solve it for you, and then snooze away.

Next morning when you rise, and before you do anything else, dash out whatever dreams you can remember. (It helps to review these dreams in your mind as you're waking up, but try not to add a running commentary. The "verbal" is Lefty's domain.)

Stay with this exercise for a while, writing what you remember without pausing to edit or even to express the ideas cogently. Shards, bits and pieces, impressions, lines of dialog—however fractured or surreal something seems, write it all down. This activity will spur the memory train to keep chugging along, dragging behind it a trail of dream images. When an image flashes on your mental screen, get it down. Then say what the image reminds you of, followed by what *that* made you think of, and so on— in a sort of free association.

Your left brain is going to fight this tooth and nail. It's been asleep all night. It wants to be up and awake and about the job of making the coffee and forecasting the weather and dreading the rest of the day. It will say things like, "This is so stupid! What earthly good is a *talking dog* in a story about World War I? That's just crazy talk. You're *dreaming,* Bub."

Meanwhile, Righty is jumping up and down, shouting, "The talking dog? That was me! I came up with that! Wasn't it great?"

Sometimes you'll have to go through this kind of back and forth before the answer to your problem "pops" from the background noise and makes itself understood. Righty sometimes has a tendency to mush things together, resulting in a weird, nonsensical narrative. But other times you'll awaken with the answer right in the forefront of your awareness.

"Oh yeah, I get it! The soldier hears a wounded man in the trench, howling like a dog, who tells him where the enemy troops were spotted."

Your right brain is making up stories *all the time*. They're the stuff dreams are made of. Make the best use of Righty's talent, and don't shoot down his strange ideas immediately. See where they take you. Upon examination, they may provide exactly what you need for your story.

Caution: It's not really a caution but I felt I should say that, anyway. Righty's a bit of a plagiarist himself. You may begin to notice that he'll slip into the future, proudly bringing home events from the next day or the next week like a tomcat with a bird in its mouth, presenting them as his own ideas.

This precognition is a normal consequence of your mind's expansion, and something that has been known to happen in meditators from the time of Patanjali, the original Yoga dude.

Back to the future!

End Experiment

12

Soul Sister

*N*ot long after moving into the Dream Cottage, I ran across a woman I hadn't seen in some years. We had a mutual friend, but had never been close ourselves. Claudia Hoover and I would spend the next ten years exploring consciousness together. It's one thing to be doing all of this reading, meditating, and experimentation on your own; it's another to have a buddy to share it with. Someone who can check your excesses or cheer your triumphs. Most importantly, someone who believes the same things you believe and doesn't think you belong in a rubber room.

Early on in the new friendship, Claudia came to the house to pick me up for dinner. "This place is so cute!" she said. "How'd you find it?" Before I could censor myself, the answer popped out: "I prayed for it."

She cocked her head—intrigued, or maybe afraid I was going to start talking Jesus. I quickly changed the subject and we went on with our evening as if nothing had been said.

On another occasion, we got together for breakfast at Rae's on Pico Boulevard. Claudia explained that she'd just been to visit her girlfriend's family back east. (This was my first inkling that she was a Lesbic-American; I cringed when I remembered trying to fix her up with a male co-worker years before.)

Somehow we got onto the subject of religion. A lapsed Catholic, Claudia felt the need for some sort of belief system, but couldn't imagine going back to a church that condemned her choice of mate. Her friend Jack was a Buddhist, she told me. Maybe she would look into that.

I started talking to her about quantum physics, explaining how our minds are constantly interacting with the environment and affecting reality. I suggested that she might like to attend my metaphysical church, but I didn't think it was a likely prospect. At any rate, I wasn't trying to proselytize. I wasn't confident enough in the teaching to do so.

The next get-together was lunch at La Frite on Ventura Boulevard. Claudia was in horrible shape. Dead broke, her career stalled. Here was a woman with an economics degree who had charmed her way into the film business to work as an editor, and within a few short years had won the Filmmaker's Trophy at the Sundance Film Festival for a documentary called *Metamorphosis*. She'd also directed several independent features, working with big-name talent like Charlton Heston and Shelley Winters. Then suddenly, everything had come to a screeching halt. There were no jobs on the horizon. She had only $120 in her bank account and $600 in unpaid bills sitting on her desk. Desperation was setting in as she neared the dreaded age of forty.

She looked me straight in the eye. "Okay, what do I do? Just tell me what to do!"

Emboldened by her despair, I said something outrageous. (Either that, or someone else was doing the talking for me):

"First of all, you're not allowed to worry about money *ever again.*"

She blinked a few times, but didn't slug me. "Okay. Only…what do I *do?*"

This time I gave her a crash course in Religious Science. I told her that she should sit in meditation and imagine herself in a financially sound position. She didn't need to know where the money was coming from, she only had to believe that it was a *fait accompli*. She should cultivate a sense of gladness over being alive, a deep-seated gratitude for all of her blessings—good looks and health, family and friends—extending that attitude to her work life, as well. If she wanted, she could use David Walker's image of a clothesline where all of her desires were hanging, just waiting for her to reel them in.

Claudia took to the philosophy like a duck to water, confirming my suspicion that desperate people make the best Truth students. She did exactly as instructed. Two days later someone called offering her an editing job. When she asked how the production people had gotten her name, she was told they had opened up the Hollywood Directory and called the first person listed in the A's, a woman who'd worked with years prior and recommended her for the job. Then someone else called with a second job offer, and then a third one came in. Obviously she couldn't take them all, but the shows' schedules were magically rearranged, allowing her to do the three jobs in succession.

She was off and running. I referred to her as The Petri Dish because, 1) She's a dishy blonde, and, 2) I was experimenting with this philosophy using her as a proxy. I was the theoretician, she was the one who took action—my Ralph Waldo Emerson to her Henry David Thoreau.

In short order, she became an editor on *Survivor*, for which she was nominated for an Emmy; she went on to edit the final episode of *Joe Millionaire*—one of the most widely viewed half-hours in the history of television; she and her girlfriend entered into a domestic partnership, left their one-bedroom apartment, bought a lovely house in a nice neighborhood, and then her partner gave birth to a beautiful baby boy. It was all so fast it made my head spin.

Claudia was so good at manifesting, so fearless and faith-filled, that I jokingly began calling her a witch. One day she was accosted at the mall by a woman handing out tickets to a tennis tournament. A sports fanatic, Claudia readily accepted the tickets, and while at the tournament, she entered a raffle. The prize was two more tickets to the semi-finals.

Claudia won the raffle.

She went to the semi-finals and entered yet *another* raffle. The prize for this one was an all expenses paid trip to Malaysia.

What do you think happened?

Amazingly, Claudia won that raffle, too—her second in a row, receiving a first-class trip as the prize. But that wasn't to be her last free trip abroad. As crazy as this sounds, I swear on my life it's true:

By the time she attended another tournament in Manhattan Beach two years later, Claudia had been a practicing Religious Scientist for some time. Even so, she didn't plan on buying a raffle ticket at this one. The odds against winning again were incalculable. Nevertheless, as she was leaving the house, her partner called out to her, "Now, what are we going to remember to do?"

Claudia said, "Wear sunscreen?"

"No, buy a raffle ticket."

Claudia responded *Yeah, sure,* but she wasn't about to waste a dollar. In the end she decided to honor her girlfriend's wishes because she didn't want any grief about it when she got home.

But she almost forgot, running over to the guy with the raffle box at the last minute. As she bought her ticket she kidded with him about the prize, which was a trip to Japan: "Is the airline ticket first-class? Because I traveled first class to Malaysia when I won my last raffle and I'd like to do it again this time."

He laughed and dropped her entry into the box. Here's the excerpt from my journal shortly afterward:

Yesterday was really something. Claudia calls up and leaves the message that when she was at the women's tennis tournament, she won a trip to Japan!

It's just so amazing, and it is proof! I told Claudia that if she needed any <u>further</u> proof, then God bless her. This, after getting nominated for an Emmy for doing a show she took just to pay the bills.

Not only was her win outrageous the second time in a row, there were some bizarre synchronicities as icing on the cake. Her family name was Hoover; Hoover Vacuum Cleaners sponsored the event. The event occurred on the 7th of the month. As she was talking to me on the phone, she saw a vanity license plate on a car in front of her that read "Hoover 7."

You couldn't make this stuff up! If you did, you'd be lambasted for foisting such unbelievable coincidences on the reading public. No one would accept it in a piece of fiction because it's too improbable.

The problem is, *it happened.*

Nor does it stop there. The Claudia juggernaut chugged on. She attended a wedding in Las Vegas not long after winning the raffle. When the wedding was over, she passed a slot machine on her way out the door. Sliding a coin into the machine, she thought, "I'm going to need some walking around money in Japan." The machine obliged with a jackpot of $2,500.

And yet, despite this run of unbelievable good fortune, the worm was about to turn. The next month Claudia and her partner attended the Emmys, dressed to the nines in evening gowns loaned to them by a costumer friend. She didn't win, but hey—isn't it supposed to be an honor just to be nominated? (Especially when you've been broke and desperate only a few months before?) Miss Thing didn't think so, and she paid the price:

Ltg 09-10-01

Claudia didn't win the Emmy. Said she shook her head throughout the ceremony. Then she went out the next morning and her car wouldn't start. Turns out she drained all the electricity from her new battery with her negativity. Also, her toilet overflowed as she was partying pre-Emmy.

She told me that after Tyne Daley won her first Emmy, her toilet exploded, which brought her back down to earth. Claudia had been thinking about that story all week…

Being a witch cuts both ways, apparently. If you're in the winning zone, you can't lose. If you're in a cranky mood, you can end up with a dead car engine or a busted toilet.

If instead of being angry, she'd been genuinely happy for the winners while continuing to desire an Emmy for herself, I believe it would have happened eventually—maybe even the following year. Now, after practicing Religious Science for a decade, I'm sure she'd agree.

I could write a whole book about Claudia, but that might get me in hot water. She has plans to write her own spiritual-memoir-that-isn't-really-a-memoir some day, so just consider this a preview of coming attractions.

Like a lot of other people in 2010, Claudia's having a tough time of it. The entertainment business has almost fallen off the map. Knowing her as I do, I can attest that when her back's up against the wall she steps on the spiritual gas and makes things happen. I look forward to watching her rebound, and I plan to be holding onto her cape when she does.[*]

Oh, what the heck, I'll include the update. One morning in September Claudia called on her way home from church. She had racked up a lot of debt since her last job ended and things were looking dire, she reported cheerfully.

As it happened, just before she called, Rajeev had received a job posting for an editor in his email. He read it out loud to me because he thought the ad was worded funny. I said, "Why don't you send that to Claudia?"

Claudia phoned only moments later, and I told her to look for the email when she returned home. She called and got the job within five minutes, earning $3,000 a week. All was right with the world once again, in no time at all.

Bippity boppity boo!

Besides being a freak show of manifesting, Claudia became my biggest cheerleader and toughest taskmaster. I'd talked about wanting to write a mystery series for a long time, but I was malingering—too afraid to start. Fiction was very far

---

[*] Or her broomstick.

outside my area of expertise, and I hadn't done all that well *in* my area of expertise.

Books were long. They had a lot of words. You couldn't just *cut* from a scene when it got messy, you needed a smooth transition from one scene to another. Couldn't leave the costume details to the wardrobe department, there wasn't any. No production designer to decorate the room and stock it with furniture. No music or sound effects to set the mood. No cinematographer to shoot the scene in an evocative style…

You had to do all of those jobs, yourself.

It was a daunting prospect, but Claudia wouldn't let me off the hook. Nor would she countenance any "I don't know how" talk from me.

"You know how," she said. "Just ask God for help. Now you and God go get busy!"

Tip: Get a consciousness buddy.[*]

If you ask the universe for a companion to come along with you on your spiritual journey, it will happen.

---

[*] Sorry, Claudia's taken.

Your desire will be telegraphed out into the noosphere and end up attracting someone new into your life.

Make sure it's someone who's open-minded, honest, imaginative, and compassionate—non-judgmental in character, easy-going in temperament.

This is someone you should be able to sit with at Starbucks, drinking coffee and planning your month-long vacation in Tuscany together, even though you're both flat broke. Not the sort of person to say, "You're not dealing with reality." But, "How about a nice wine pairing with that fresh prosciutto?"

Not, "Do you *know* how many women directors there are actually working in Hollywood?" but, "Can you make sure they offer some low-carb lunches when we're hanging on the set of your movie?"

You'll be sharing your deepest desires with this person, along with the belief that those desires will come about. They'll be reflecting your beliefs back to you.

This will result in a loop of thought that has all the more power to manifest, and will make you feel a lot less crazy.

End Tip

Experiment: Send your buddy a telepathic request to call you.

Try this several times, and take note of the lag time between the moment you send out the message and the moment you hear the blaring of your ringtone.

Telepathy tends to develop between like-minded people who spend a lot of time together. You've probably already experienced something like this before, and now you know why: Your mind is not limited to the space between your ears.

Reach out with it and touch someone!

End Experiment

13

Miracle Contagion

*E*veryone knows the story of the four-minute mile. For the longest time four minutes was considered to be an unbreakable record. Then someone beat it, and suddenly everyone and his brother was blasting over that hurdle. It wasn't a physical barrier that had prevented people from achieving it but a mental one.

Once you see someone do something new, an avenue of possibility opens up in your mind. If you formerly believed a thing was impossible and then you see it occur, your mind has to grapple with a whole new reality in which it *is* possible. At this juncture, it has two choices: It can either accept the new set of circumstances, stretching out to accommodate them, or it can shut itself down for self-protection.

Some people just can't adjust. They won't even let physical proof of an event alter their worldview, so threatened are they by the implications.

But remember the Whack-a-Moles, my friends, the miracles that will start popping up all over the place once you allow them to!

This chapter will illustrate how whatever we hold in consciousness has a tendency to appear in our experience, as well as showing that wonders can be accomplished by a monkey-see, monkey-do phenomenon I call a "miracle contagion." If you're the sort who's prone to saying "I never win anything," please pay close attention to the following story.

Claudia had just won her second free trip. When I told my little sister about it, she got steamed. "That witch! Dammit, *I* want to win something!"

She went to Target soon afterward, pushing her new baby in a stroller. As she entered the front door she saw a large cardboard cutout of a motor-scooter. They were having a drawing with the scooter for a prize.

I'm going to win that, thinks she.

Determined to show Claudia who was the better witch, she rolled the poor kid all over the store looking for a form to fill out. Finally, she found the display at the very back, hidden away from the high-traffic areas. While the baby sat in his wet diaper—*Sorry, honey. Mommy's obsessed with showing up someone else's mommy!*[*]—she ripped off the form, filled it out, and dropped it in the slot. Then she went on about her business.

---

[*] I made that up to tweak her out. *Hi, sweetie!*

A week later she got the call from Target to pick up her shiny new Vespa. It's red—how's that for a magic color? Her pride and joy is now collecting dust in the garage, a testament to her witchiness.

Did this change her into a believer overnight? No, she rationalized that because the entry forms were so far out of sight, she'd probably been the only one to enter the drawing.

Ahem, you're missing the point, Sis:

You decided to win something and you did almost immediately, no matter how it came about!

After hearing about Claudia's good fortune she decided to win something, too. She happened to go to Target where— guess what?—they were having a drawing. A drawing that only one determined little lady with a stroller would be able to locate. She trekked all over the store to find that display, then spelled her name correctly and got her phone number right, and that was all that was needed to win an expensive prize.

All it takes is a made-up mind.

I call this beginner's luck. The first time a prayer is answered so effortlessly it can freak you out. Afterward, you diminish your miracle-making power by trying to rationalize the occurrence away.

Never look a miracle in the mouth. Just say thank you and move on.

The fact is that **BIG-ASS MIRACLES** will frequently come in a way that makes sense to us in some form or fashion, offering us plausible deniability when they occur: *Move along! Nothing to see here, just some darn good luck!*

If we could accept things materializing out of thin air from another dimension, they probably would. But we can't, so we're presented with stories that make the miracle palatable. If it's *too* uncanny, it gives the lie to the larger picture—that of a solid, mechanistic world that works according to established rules. Most people aren't prepared to accept a reality in which that's not the case, unless the occurrence is at Lourdes or some other legendary place. I'm not trying to say that the world *doesn't* work according to rules, just that those rules were made to be broken on occasion.

The idea is to live in this reality with the understanding that there are things at work that can't be seen with the naked eye nor understood with the reasoning mind. When you walk into a situation without fear or reservation, you present a clear channel for God to come through. My sister's desire was strong and pure—not because she was *had* to win something in order to survive, although that can be a strong motivator—but simply because she wanted it.

For fun.

To prove she could.

Doesn't matter the reason!

I know as well as anyone that it's impossible to stay in this "miracle mindset" all of the time. This is planet Earth, not the Holodeck on the Starship Enterprise. The thing is, you don't *have* to stay in it all the time. If you can muster fifty-one percent belief, that will put you over the edge.

Because I've witnessed the working of miracle contagions on many occasions, I now believe that talking about miracles, writing about them, thinking about them, and watching people perform them makes it possible for others to experience them too.

In other words, merely the act of reading of this book can make extraordinary things possible in your own experience.

A miracle for the price of a book? *Not a bad deal.*

Tip: Imagine you are a genie. Or Jeannie. Or Harry Potter.

Metaphysical writer Florence Scovel Shinn wrote a book called *Your Word is Your Wand.* Her approach to the subject matter was fun and whimsical.

Florence said that the more playful you are with this process, the better off you'll be. Pretend, just like a child. Take the attitude that you're involved in a mind game.

People are frequently more successful at materializing trivial things because they haven't injected their Inner Naysayer into the process, not having much emotional investment in, say, whether they get a parking space directly in front of the dry cleaner's. But when there's more on the line, like financial issues or matters of the heart, those critical voices will pipe up—the ghostly intonations of parents or preachers or homeroom teachers, telling you this manifestation stuff is all childish nonsense.

You can fight those voices. Shoot back with: "It's a game, that's all. So are tennis and golf and football, and people have fun playing those. Where's the harm?

We're 'feeling the crazy' and doing it anyway! Who cares if it's all imaginary *bulls*—Whoa. Was that a large check that just showed up in the mail...? I wasn't expecting that. *Spooky...*"

Your word *is* your wand. Use it wisely, Master Potter. Above all, have fun with it.

End Tip

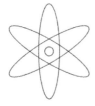

Experiment: Be a Bonanza Magnet!

After her experience winning the scooter, my sister decided to adopt the attitude that she "always" won drawings. Soon thereafter, she was the proud new owner of a Flip Camera, the prize for a raffle held at one of her business luncheons. She told me that as they were about to make the announcement, she heard her own name called twice—first in her mind, then from the mouth of the emcee.

Enter every drawing and contest you come across. Do it in the spirit of fun, with no attachment to the outcome.

Instead of saying "I never win anything," try thinking: "Isn't it great that I'm always winning things?" Then give a big *Mwah!* to the Universe in advance for showering you with its bounty.

On *The Ellen Show* one afternoon, they were giving away prizes to audience members who'd won a drawing held before the show was taped. One young woman had actually tried to decline Ellen's prizes.

The reason?

She didn't want to be greedy, having just won a multimillion Lottery jackpot. They brought her up on stage with her giant check as proof. Talk about being in the winning zone—this girl was some kind of *bonanza magnet.*

Make up your mind to be one, too.

This stuff works! It really, really works!

End Experiment

14

Books are Looooong

*I*t was time for a miracle in my own life, but first I had to decide what it should look like. Though I knew I wanted to write a mystery novel, I didn't know quite how to start.

In summer of 2001, I saw a documentary about three famous writers called *Women of Mystery*. Featured in the film were Sue Grafton, whose "alphabet" books star private detective Kinsey Milhone; Sara Paretsky (private eye V.I. Warshawski); and Marcia Muller (PI Sharon McCone). I found myself really envying those lady authors. I wanted to be sitting in a writing loft weaving mystery stories for an adoring public, a dog at my feet, cup of tea at my elbow.

Around that time, I missed a reunion in Texas with two of my girlfriends. When I called one of them to express regrets, telling her about my plan to write mysteries, she uttered the fateful words, "Have you ever heard of Janet Evanovich?"

The Stephanie Plum novels were a revelation. As soon as I read them, I knew I had my role model. I kept saying to myself, "I didn't know you could do things like this in a book!" I'd always believed that published novels had to be at least somewhat literary, but these were funny as hell and written like screenplays, with lots of action and whole pages of dialogue. I devoured all that were available at the time, numbers one through six.

But I still had no idea how to write a narrative (one abortive attempt at a romance novel, notwithstanding). Having trained myself in the kind of minimalist storytelling that screenplays require, I didn't really know how to fill a page, how to describe characters in detail, how to set a scene. When a story analyst sees too much type in a screenplay, she thinks you don't know what you're doing and automatically rejects the script. The ideal screenplay has lots and lots of empty space to be filled with the visuals that will ultimately appear on the screen.

I decided to learn on the fly. The book would take place in Beverly Hills, because anything with "Beverly Hills" in the title sells. And how do the rich, beautiful Beverly Hills people fill their time? They have plastic surgery, trying to be even *more* rich and beautiful looking, making them excellent fodder for satire. Thus I had my setting and the backdrop to the action.

My protagonist would be a female private eye. The PI had to have a sidekick—someone to act as a sounding board as well as a foil, maybe even someone more interesting than the lead herself. An outrageous TYPE who would provide a different perspective and most of the laughs.

From my reading in the genre, it seemed that all the good sidekicks were taken. I wanted something original, but was there anything new under the sun?

Lying on The Magic Bed, I stared at the ceiling, waiting for the answer. After a time, I reached that hypnagogic state that is part of the meditation process, and the answer came to me, clear as a bell:

Identical twins.

"Genius!" I shot up off the bed. "It's completely original. No one's ever done that before!"

Sometimes when you travel to the realm of the right brain, you come back a little foggy. When the excitement wore off a few minutes later, I remembered that there *had* been a successful mystery series using a similar device. Perhaps you've heard of them?

The Bobbsey Twins.

I'd never read those books, so maybe I can be forgiven for forgetting about them. But immediately on the heels of that realization was: "How about those friggin' Hardy Boys? Were they twins, too?"

Turns out that The Hardy Boys were regular brothers. And the Bobbseys, I discovered, were two sets of *fraternal* twins, not identical ones. Plus, they looked like *Dick and Jane*, which meant they were older than dirt. There may be nothing new under the sun, but people only live so long, which means you can recycle ideas every couple of generations.

Anxious to start, I was nevertheless daunted by the undertaking. The self-doubt was returning full force. I fought back my insecurity long enough to start envisioning the twins and fleshing out their characters. They would be hot redheads, I decided—opposites, despite their indistinguishable looks, mirror images in every respect. The narrator Kerry would be the older sister by a minute and a half and heterosexual; the younger sister Terry would be gay.

Kerry would be right-handed; Terry, a lefty. Kerry a straight-A student; Terry, dyslexic. Kerry, a fearful, law-abiding type; Terry, a daredevil with addiction issues. These two diametrically opposed lookalikes would ride around Los Angeles on a hot-pink Harley solving crimes.

That's how the McAfee Twins came into the world.

I wasn't consciously aware of creating characters that represented the two sides of the personality, the ego and the id; I just thought it would be a fun contrast. Terry represents the shadow side of Kerry's nature, and Kerry complains bitterly that might have turned out to be an adventurous person herself, if she hadn't had to watch out for her impulsive little sister.

When my friend Jim heard about the characters, he said, "You'll save yourself thousands in therapy."

"Too late for that," I assured him.

I had my protagonists and my location, so I asked around for scoop on plastic surgeons. A friend of my sister's, an ophthalmic surgeon, told me a doozy of a true story:

Once upon a time there was a plastic surgeon in Texas. The doctor had been dipping into the painkillers, and one day he got the bright idea to give himself an eyelift. Looking in the mirror, he sliced his own eyelids to remove the excess skin, with the unfortunate result that he took too much flesh. This left him unable to close his eyes, necessitating a constant flow of drops, and his wide-open stare was frightening to behold.

The kicker to the story was that the doctor was investigated by the Texas Medical Board, who ruled that he was fit to continue practicing medicine. (Foxes guarding the henhouse, anyone?)

This story of vanity and insanity was the perfect inspiration for my story. I created a Beverly Hills cosmetic surgeon who runs an illegal prescription drug ring, using his elderly female patients as street merchants in a kind of twisted pyramid marketing scheme. Terry refers to these drug-addled old ladies as the "Mary Kays from Hell."

But by August 22nd I still hadn't written anything:

> Ltg 08-22-01
>
> Walking through the bookstore the other day, I was intimidated by how many books there were on the shelves, and how few of the authors I'd actually heard of. Then it occurred to me—this isn't so many, considering a population of 300 million. And I'm going to be among their ranks.
>
> Why? Because I prayed for it. Because I asserted it in Mind. And I can wait, because there is no waiting. There's no yesterday, today or tomorrow. It's all here now.

It was almost three months since I'd seen the documentary, and still no novel. Then came September 11th 2001. I made no journal entry on that day, instead leaving only a blank page with the date as a header. I still can't put my feelings into words except as a string of nouns:

Horror, shock, despair, depression, hopelessness, dread.

More than those buildings had come down in my mind; a way of life seemed to be ending. One thing I've always loved about American culture is the premium we place on humor. We've kept our leaders in their place by making fun of them, like a country of court jesters holding the king's clay feet to the fire.

In the wake of that horrible event, I wondered if we would ever regain our national sense of humor. Would satire even be tolerated in the age of The Patriot Act?

Only time would tell, but I comforted myself with the knowledge that a lot of great music, theater, comedy, and literature has been created during times of war. Art outlasts all of the tyrants, politicos, fanatics, and the conflicts they create. It's what we have left when the dust settles.

I pulled myself out of depression by reading comedy, and by watching humorists like Jon Stewart spoof the powers that be. Humor was the salve my siblings and I had always used to soothe the pain of loss, and it worked again this time.

You've heard the definitions of comedy and tragedy? Tragedy is when stuff happens, nobody changes, then everybody dies. Comedy is when stuff happens, nobody changes, but everything works out all right in the end. I like to think that people can change their consciousness and thereby improve the state of the world, but until they do, humor may be the best defense against the madness. It's hard to create drama when you're laughing your ass off.

Although it's fair to say that nothing *has* been the same since September 11th, by November of that year I was feeling more optimistic:

Ltg 11-10-01

I am a comic crime novelist, a best-selling comic/crime novelist. I know I can do this, and I'm gonna.

The Miramax money wasn't going to last forever. I began to think about getting a freelance job I could do while continuing to write books. Riveted by courthouse action ever since the Menendez and Simpson trials, I was constantly tuned into Court TV. I decided to investigate the field of court reporting. The profession paid well and could certainly be a source of material for future crime novels. I even went so far as to attend an open house at the Bryan School of Court Reporting (yes the same folks who advertise on cable TV), where I learned to my dismay that it would take four whole years to become accredited.

How many books could I write in four years? I decided to stick to novels and let God sort out my finances.

Ltg 12-06-01

Thou shalt not be anxious.

Yesterday asked myself, Would you be anxious if you knew you were a successful writer? Answer: no. So why be anxious, because you are a successful writer!

Bought six books on how to write mysteries. Pretty sure I can do this. Excuse me, it's already done.

Before starting, I taught myself about the structure of comic mysteries by dissecting Janet Evanovich's novels. In an Excel spreadsheet, I made notes on the contents of each chapter, including the character arcs, the A, B, C, and D stories, and the number of laugh-out-loud jokes per page.

After getting a feel for structure, I finally began to write *The Butcher of Beverly Hills*. Within sixty days I had a rambling, disjointed, and unfunny manuscript that I enthusiastically foisted on my friend and relatives to get their notes. This is how I learned that you should never ask anyone to read a first draft. They were kind but firm. It needed to be cut back. It had the "germ" of a good story. There were funny bits but they didn't cohere. The bad guy was not believable. The ending seemed contrived.

What a downer. I had been ecstatic to write the words THE END, so pleased to have been able to print out that big stack of paper. But the truth was that I had the bulk of the work still ahead of me.

A few drafts later, I queried an agent who was excited to read the manuscript, being a twin herself. She insisted that I send it to her via Federal Express so she could take it with her to New York. Weeks later she wrote back, saying that it needed to be trimmed. She encouraged me to keep at it.

I did, working ten to twelve hours a day. My back ached, my eyesight declined. Dishes were growing mold in the sink. Black cat dander lay in drifts up to the windowsills. I lived in constant fear of the Animal Welfare people sending a SWAT team to bust in and rescue the kitties from their squalid living conditions.

Finally, after several more drafts, *Butcher* began to resemble a polished manuscript.

A process emerged that would hold for each of my subsequent books. First I write a "something/anything draft," throwing everything up onto the screen that enters my mind, to be cleaned up and organized later.

When there are enough words (usually 50,000 – 70,000), I start a spreadsheet listing the main story points and character developments, as I'd done while deconstructing Janet's books. Using varying color highlights, I track the main story and the subplots. A plotline featuring the secondary characters, Aunt Reba and Cousin Robert, will have its own story arc that develops in tandem with the main story, usually climaxing just after the central mystery does. The romantic subplot is graphed in the same way. I chart the red herrings, those diversions you create to lead the reader away from the ultimate bad guy, making sure there are plenty of possible villains.

During this phase, the main story begins to stand out from the rest, allowing me to concentrate on the spine of the book. Large chunks of material that slow down the action are trimmed. The characters' motivations are brought into focus by asking at each point in the story: *What is he/she thinking right now? What does he/she want out of this scene?*

Then I go on "Extra Word Patrol," cutting unnecessary modifiers to tighten the prose. Transitions between chapters are smoothed out. When I feel a passage or line of dialogue should be funnier, I stare at the page until a better joke occurs to me.

At this point, I nail down the ending for good. Whereas I may have started out with a idea of what it would be, a new solution to the mystery can sometimes appear, developing out of clues I've unconsciously planted in earlier chapters. When "whodunnit" is a mystery even to me, it's more likely to surprise the reader, as well.

Ltg 05-20-02

MY MIND'S MADE UP.

I've conveyed to my unconscious and to Divine Mind that I need a perfect rewrite of the book, with narrative drive that keeps you guessing and keeps you interested, and a perfect resolution to the story, and a perfect resonance of the theme.

Finally, I began to look for an agent again. I went to the websites of other writers and read about the process—how to compose a query letter, how to submit to an agent, how long to wait until you give up. There were no comprehensive listings of agents on the Web at that time, so I photocopied pages from the *Guide to Literary Agents* in the reference section of the library.

Of the dozen or so that I queried, none was interested. Claudia insisted that I approach Janet Evanovich's agent. Claudia can be very ~~bossy~~ persuasive, so after hearing this for a while, I went ahead and located the agent's name in the acknowledgments section of one of Janet's books. I wrote him a query letter and he wrote back, respectfully declining.

I began to wonder if the whole thing was going to be a wash-out. Claudia insisted I would make good if I kept the faith:

Ltg 05-22-02

At lunch with Claudia I asked the question, "Do our thoughts and desires override everyone else's thoughts and desires, just because we're using our thought consciously?"

She said, "You're sitting around treating for a publishing deal. That means your thought is going to affect a load of people in the publishing industry, who thus far have never heard of you and haven't read your stuff. Then your thought is going to affect thousands of people who will read your books. What do you call that?"

A stunning answer, and it has to be the truth if we believe what we believe.

The deadlines were coming up for two prestigious contests: the Private Eye Writers of America/St. Martin's Press

Best First Private Eye Novel, and one sponsored by the Crime Writers Association in England. The first prize in the PWA contest was a publishing contract with St. Martin's. The British contest was exclusively about recognition.

I entered both and meditated on winning them, visualizing going to England to accept one prize, being interviewed about my new publishing deal with St. Martin's after winning the other.

The finalists of the U.K. contest were to be published on their website. The PWA/St. Martin's announcement would arrive by mail on September 16th. Every day I checked the status of the CWA contest online, and visualized going out to the mailbox and opening my notification from St. Martin's, while I continued to pump myself up in the journal.

Ltg 09-10-02

Another day of JUST TODAY.

Just today I'm going to truly believe in the Principle of Mind. Just today I'm going to really believe that my thought creates my experience. Just today I'm going to really feel that success is mine. That money is no longer an issue, ever. That my life is completely blessed, and I am GUARANTEED a return on my investment in positive thought.

I have a publishing deal, a lucrative one. I have the perfect editor. I have what everybody says you can't have in the publishing world—SUCCESS AS A NEW WRITER.

126

The announcement days came and went. I continued to insist that I *had* won. Another week went by, then two. Despite the insanity of persisting, I kept up my affirmations, reminding myself that there was no past, present, future—imagining that my current thinking could and would somehow affect the "past."

When six weeks had gone by, I finally gave up—on the contests, at least. My name had not appeared on the CWA website, nor had I heard from St. Martin's. While Rajeev was away working on a film in the Bay Area, I got busy researching self-publishing. After buying a domain name, I set out to launch a crude website to promote the book. Sister was doing it for herself because Sister had had it with rejection.

When Rajeev returned home, he was surprised to learn I'd made a deal with iUniverse. The digital revolution was something he'd never imagined me taking part in, but I'd jumped in feet first. The manuscript had already been submitted and they were working on a cover.

Meanwhile, I sent the book out for review to *All About Murder*, a Yahoo mystery fan group. The reviewer claimed she needed to wear Depends because she was laughing so hard—high praise for a comedy writer. I brought the review to lunch at a Mexican restaurant so I could read it over and over again. Rajeev asked if I was planning to have it tattooed on my body.

He lent his expertise in launching the site, and we were in the process of doing just that when a package arrived with a return address of St. Martin's Press in New York. Opening the envelope, I stared at its contents in confusion.

It was my *Butcher* manuscript. (They had explicitly stated that no manuscripts would be returned to those who didn't win.) In the enclosed letter, a senior editor congratulated me on being a finalist, while apologizing for the delay in notifying me.

Occupied with thoughts of the website, and still very confused, I tossed the letter away muttering, "Well, at least I didn't finish last."

It took me a few minutes and the reaction of my husband to realize: *Hey, I didn't just "not lose," I was a finalist!* The editor stated that there were a number of fine books submitted to the contest, and to be among the finalists should be considered an honor.

My manuscript had placed in a very prestigious contest. Surely that would get me noticed by agents. The self-publishing was not supposed to be an end in itself but a means to getting published. I still planned on having an agent one day. I wondered if there would be an announcement about this contest in *Publishers Weekly,* which would be a nice addition to my query letter.

I called St. Martin's and was connected with an editor who was involved with the competition. I asked him how many manuscripts had been submitted. He told me it was in the hundreds. How many finalists were there? Around ten, he thought. I asked if they would be publishing the names of the finalists, online or in print? No, they wouldn't be doing that, he said testily. When I asked how I could verify to agents that I'd actually been a finalist, he said, "Well, you've got your letter."

Next I wrote to the president of the Private Eye Writers of America asking if *they* were going to publicize the finalists. He flew into a snit, lecturing me on how "you new, young writers with your *web-sites* think you can shortcut your way into the publishing business!" He all but called me a whippersnapper, even implying that I had broken the rules of the contest by entering a published book.

I explained that the book was unpublished when I *entered*, and that I might not have self-published at all if it hadn't been two months before I'd heard from them about being a finalist—adding that I was neither young nor new, but *thanks for the thought.*

Why was everyone treating me like a gadfly? Why offer up a contest at all if not to provide encouragement to the people who place in it? I was truly baffled by these reactions.

Claudia insisted I go back to Janet's agent with this information. To appease her, I did, and received another polite rejection. Around this time, more and more agents were visible online. I'd run across a woman named Jenny Bent who looked like a comer, but her website said that she wouldn't take unsolicited manuscripts. *Too bad*, I thought. *She looks really cool.* I didn't realize it was up to me to solicit her.

I'd previously found inspiration in a comic essayist named Laurie Notaro, who had jumped off the agent merry-go-round and published herself through iUniverse. Afterward she was picked up by Random House for a six-figure publishing deal. *And what do you know?* Her agent turned out to be Jenny Bent.

Finally, I received some good news. A big New York agent answered my query, asking me to send *Butcher* to her via Federal Express. She called me ten minutes after the package hit her doorstep. I know because I'd just checked the FedEx website to see if it had arrived. She said she liked what she'd read so far and wanted to know about the self-publishing aspect—were the rights to the book unencumbered?

iUniverse's stated policy was they would *consider* letting you out of the contract if there was interest from a publisher. Stretching the truth—but relying on the Truth—I assured her it would be no problem. She promised to get back to me soon.

On the advice of my sisters, I waited a month to hear, constantly affirming that I had the perfect agent. Finally, I wrote the woman an email asking what she thought of the manuscript. I referenced the title in the email, which I still have in my archives. This was her verbatim response:

"what are you talking about"

No greeting, no signature, no capitalization, to say nothing of punctuation. Who was she, The Incredible Hulk? I wrote back and explained that we'd spoken a month earlier and reminded her of the title of the book, which had been in the body of my email in the first place. I received another email from her two weeks later:

"Thank you for your email. We are not enthusiastic enough about the book to feel we are the right agents for you. Best of luck."

At least she used complete sentences to reject me.

I began writing a second book in the series, *The Mangler of Malibu Canyon.* Surprisingly, I found that the second book was even harder to write than the first. I must have learned something while writing *Butcher*, so why was this so *bleeping* difficult? I already knew the characters. Working with the same people in a new scenario should be at least marginally easier, no? Didn't turn out to be that way.

I began a practice of writing letters to myself in the future:

Ltg 01-18-03

Dear Future Self (Re: Mangler):

This first draft stuff is hard. Remember that. I looked at the story point spreads that I had done on Butcher and they IN NO WAY resemble the end product. I was all over the place the first couple of drafts. THEN I found the story and was able to make it work, so...

Don't worry if it's absolute crap the first time through...it doesn't matter if it makes no sense, has no narrative drive, and there's nothing too funny in it...

YOU'LL FIX IT!

Love,

Me

When I told Rajeev about this, he teased me mercilessly: "Woo-hoo, I'm calling you from the *fuuuuture*...Past Self, is there anything for dinner?"

Time dragged by, with no progress on the agent front. All of my queries were turned down. For encouragement, I mocked up an announcement of my deal-to-be, taking the logo off the *Publishers Weekly* website for authenticity. This is the fake press release I wrote for Future Self's future deal on October 13, 2003:

PUBLISHERS WEEKLY © Reed Business Information

The McAfees Ride

NEWS > HOT DEALS > 2004

Comic mystery maven Jennifer Colt has signed a six-figure deal for her "screwball mystery" series, starring the irrepressible McAfee twins. A spokesman for the publisher said, "Colt has created one-of-a-kind characters that jump off the page at you. Her mysteries are imaginative, wacky romps that bring to mind Janet Evanovich's Stephanie Plum series. We think the McAfee Twins have the same kind of breakout potential."

I kept the page open on my computer and read it from time to time, trying to concretize it in my mind. If it was real in my imagination it would have to occur in "reality."

By the time *Mangler* was almost finished, the screenwriting money was virtually gone. Rajeev came out of the shower one day and saw me pounding away at the keyboard. He said, more kindly than this may sound, "Positive thinking is great and everything, but maybe you should consider getting a job."

"Sure," I lied.

Instead I continued writing and looking for an agent. What kept me going were the good reviews I'd received, my placement in the PWA contest, and the determination to be a fulltime writer. The screenwriting work at Miramax had been great, but what I really wanted was to spend the rest of my life writing whatever *I* wanted to write.

It was hard not to become discouraged sometimes. Here is one of my favorite emails, received after I followed up with an agent on a submission she had requested two months previously:

> "Jennifer, yes, you're (sic) instincts are correct. [Agent's name] left [Agency] some time ago…Best of luck to you."

Jennifer, yes, you're (sic) instincts are correct: You have entered a funhouse hall of mirrors and will never find your way out. Cheers!

I self-published Mangler, then started immediately on the third book in the series, *The Vampire of Venice Beach*. The third time was supposed to be a charm, but…

> Ltg 11-24-03
>
> I'm on page 190 out of 280 in the course of a rewrite of Vampire and it SUCKS.
>
> Positively SUCKS, makes no SENSE, is BORING, all the dialog is STILTED and people are

rushing around for NO REASON, and the story is CONFUSED.

Just want this on record when I'm holding the book in my hand, published by Random House or somebody, and receiving great reviews and maybe an award or something, okay?

This process does NOT RUN SMOOTHLY. It's torture sometimes.

Did you catch the reference to Random House?

By the time I was almost finished with *The Vampire of Venice Beach*, I'd amassed enough reviews to compose a new query letter. Writing your own promo copy is hard to do because you know too much about the story, making it difficult to isolate the salient points. I overcame this problem by cribbing quotes from reviews.

After a few more rejections, I again ran across the website of that agent who had caught my eye months before, the one who wouldn't take unsolicited manuscripts. I girded my loins [*Ed.–What with, Spanx?*] and sent her the query letter anyway. It's reproduced here in its entirety because I know aspiring authors are always curious to read successful query letters.

February 3rd, 2004

Dear Ms. Bent:

I believe you when you say you're not accepting manuscripts, HOWEVER:

How could I resist pitching the woman who reps the Sweet Potato Queens and Laurie Notaro?

I'm a former screenwriter of horror and adult fare who's turned to mystery fiction (loosely defined). My first novel, The Butcher of Beverly Hills, was a finalist in the PWA/St. Martin's Press Best First Private Eye Novel Contest 2002.

I self-published Butcher and its sequel, The Mangler of Malibu Canyon, while agent-seeking. (It was Laurie Notaro's testimonial on iUniverse's website that prompted me to do it.) I'm currently at work on the third book in the series, The Vampire of Venice Beach.

Reviewers have called the books "hilarious," "delightful," "a breath of fresh air from a very funny writer." I call them "I Love Lucy-Noir."

Below is a synopsis of the series as a whole:

THE MCAFEE TWINS MYSTERIES

Imagine if the girls from The Parent Trap grew up to be PI's. [*]

Kerry and Terry McAfee are redheaded twins and fledgling investigators. They travel around on a shocking pink Harley that looks like something from the *Barbie Goes Hog Wild*! collection, out to right the wrongs of the world (or at least the wrongs of the greater Los Angeles area).

They grew up in Burbank, the daughters of a gaffer father and housewife mother. Kerry was straight A's, valedictorian, chess club. Terry was cigarettes on the blacktop and setting the principal's desk on fire. Kerry had a crush on the varsity quarterback; Terry torched for the homecoming queen.

---

[*] Stolen from a review.

Through an accident of fate, they ended up as gumshoes.

They lost their parents young. Terry took out her grief in nose candy and wound up in prison. Big sister Kerry (she's a minute and a half older) apprenticed herself to an investigator in the office of Terry's criminal attorney, Eli Weintraub, Esq.

Eventually Kerry qualified for a PI license and started her own business. When Terry got out of the hoosegow, Kerry hired her.

"Who else would?" Kerry asks. "She's dyslexic, completely resistant to authority, and has a criminal mind that approaches the genius level. Blessed with the gift of gab (some would say the gift of pathological lying), she can talk the fur off a lemur. She's also completely fearless, which causes me both envy and, well, fear."

They're not conjoined twins; theoretically they could go their separate ways. But they're emotionally bound like Chang and Eng were at the spleen. Kerry believes Terry needs looking after; Terry thinks big sis needs a regular kick in the ass.

In the year they've been in business, they've tracked down deadbeat dads, videotaped romantic interludes at the Motel 6, even conducted urine tests on Wal-Mart employees suspected of getting high on the job.

But their cases are about to get more exotic. They will uncover a prescription drug ring in Beverly Hills, infiltrate an extraterrestrial cult in Malibu, and bust a gang of vampires dealing black market blood in Venice.

And that's just for starters.

Their methods are unorthodox and they are luckier than they have a right to be, but the McAfees always get their man (or cult leader, or transsexual psycho-killer, or vampire, or Middle Eastern terrorist).

Kerry and Terry are truly heroines for our times—intrepid, smart-mouthed, and prone to the occasional pratfall. They'll have you laughing all the way to the morgue.[*]

"Not since Janet Evanovich have I read such a funny, laugh-out-loud book."

—Susan Johnson, www.myshelf.com

"I don't know where to begin reviewing The Butcher of Beverly Hills. It is that good...!"

—Sue Hartigan, member of RIO and www.allaboutmurder.com Reviews.

"Jennifer Colt has written a winner... a laugh-a-minute thrill ride."

—Angela Gibbs, www.timeless-tales.net

"...the sharp, witty voice... grabs the reader from the very first chapter and holds them hostage until the final hilarious page."

—Jennifer Apodaca, author of Dating Can Be Murder

"...one of the craziest, funniest things I have read."

—Webspinner, www.booksnbytes.com

---

[*] Stolen from a review.

I'd be happy to send you the finished manuscripts, as well as pages from the one I'm working on. Sample chapters and full reviews are available at www.jennifercolt.com.

Thank you for your consideration,

Jennifer Colt

Jenny requested all three manuscripts, saying they sounded "wonderful." For some reason, I didn't feel I was being strung along this time. I sent a big pile of paper up to her in New York—not overnight, I'd learned *that* much. The address was for a company called Trident Media Group, not The Bent Agency. Apparently she'd folded her agency into a larger one. I logged onto Trident's website, and what did I find?

They had Janet Evanovich listed among their clients. This was her current agency; the other man no longer represented her at all. I only mention this synchronicity because it was one of many. I'm not implying a one-to-one correspondence with everything I prayed for and the things that came about as a result, but these coincidences *are* interesting nonetheless.

After sending my manuscripts, I laid on The Magic Bed and meditated on the situation. I asserted over and over that I had the perfect agent. Not Jenny specifically, because I couldn't know that she was, but the perfect *representative*.

Then on March 2nd Jenny wrote back, wanting to know if I was still unrepresented. I told her I was. She asked for the sales numbers on the first two books.

Yikes.

I'd only sold about sixty *Butchers*, and even fewer *Manglers.* I'd been more interested in writing the books than marketing them, as was evident from the homemade covers. (iUniverse's *Butcher* cover was even worse, a clipart picture of a knife dripping blood.) Still, I had good reviews and she wanted to see all of them. In the absence of good sales numbers, the reviews would be important. I sent them up via email.

And waited, and waited, chewing my nails to the quick.

Oops. I meant to say *I waited in utter relaxation, with the calm expectation that what I had asked for was on its way to me.*

Yeah, that's it. I was the very picture of *calm...*

Tip: Calm yourself down with prayer and visualization.

Lie on your bed, "magic" or not, and try to relax and breathe. Remind yourself that your thought is lining up circumstances exactly the way you want them, and that the only way to stop them from happening is to have a bunch of fearful thoughts that will push them away.

Your bodymind can't tell the difference between an imagined threat and a real one. The reaction in both cases is exactly the same: sweaty palms, racing heart, adrenaline overload, constricted blood vessels.

The good news is that it can't tell the difference between a real boon and an imagined one, either. When you imagine a good outcome, your heart rate evens out, your immune system functions more efficiently, and your life will be longer and happier as a result. (Unless it's a *great* outcome, in which case your heart rate will speed up then, as well. Don't worry, great news is *always* good news for your health.)

Go for the healthier alternative. Imagine the good stuff, not the bad! And when you do, you'll be bringing more good stuff to you through the Law of Attraction.

Remember, you only have to keep yourself in line 51% of the time.

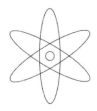

Experiment: Same as above, only quicker.

If you've never experimented with controlling your unconscious bodily functions, try this:

Think of biting into a lemon. Feel your mouth pucker, your glands going crazy, rebelling at the tanginess of it.

You've just used your imagination to create a physical reaction in your body. It's amazing to think about, but true: Your body is constantly reacting to your thoughts in exactly the same way.

Like the Tibetan monks who are famous for it, you can slow down your own heartbeat, speed up or slow down your metabolism, heal and restore your tissues and organs. You can achieve euphoria with nothing more than your thoughts.

Tell your body how you want it to feel by saying:

"Everything is perfect. Everything is going my way. Everything in life is way cool!"

It may feel like you're lying, at first; but soon, when everything starts *actually* going your way, you'll be having too much fun to care.

End Experiment

15

My Big Fat Book Deal

*B*y March 8th Jenny had read the books.

Ltg 03-09-04

GOT AN AGENT YESTERDAY!

Ms. Jenny Bent of Trident Media Group. She had left me an email in my box that I got first thing, asking me to call about representation.

She started out talking about Vampire. Said she really liked it. Thought out loud about strategy: "I can't send three manuscripts to people, they'll freak." She's thinking she'll send them Vampire, then tell them they can have the two previous ones, too.

She wants to look at the self-published books, maybe send them with the manuscript. I told her the covers were shit.

Finally, she said, "I want to represent you."

I said, "Good, because you're the one I want." I told her I'd been happy to see that she represented so many humorists.

"Yeah, I've had most of my success with that. I'm going to represent you as 'chick-lit crime'," she said, "They're not mysteries, they're crime novels. You're not a mystery writer, you're a crime novelist."

Okay by me, I said, but I put "mystery" in the title. She said that would have to come out.

She really liked the Vampire pages. She said, "What are they, is this finished?" I said I'd just sent some polished pages, that the manuscript was essentially done, but not as funny as it needs to be. I said I'd finish it in a couple of weeks.

She said, "I think people are going to be excited about these." Which, now that I think of it, means that people will pay for these. Goody.

Jenny requested copies of the iUniverse books. She also asked me to write a bio, and then after reading it, asked me to write another one. When I asked if she wanted a bio that was "non-jokey," including college education, childhood dreams, and business experience, she said yes. I did my best.

She put the books out to auction five weeks later. On April 22nd she emailed me to say, "Call me this afternoon if you can—we have two offers on your book!"

Two offers! I was apoplectic with joy. One was for a total of $30,000. It broke down as $20,000 for the third book and $5,000 for each of the first two, which they wanted to release out of order. The second offer was a straight $7,500 per manuscript.

I barely slept that night. Logging on the next morning, I found this email from Jenny:

> Jennifer,

> The offer I was expecting from Broadway looks less like a sure thing now, but if it comes, it's coming tomorrow. I'll keep you posted on any further development.

> Hugs,

> Jenny

Ltg 04-23-04

Jenny calls me ten minutes after the email. She says, "Jennifer...? Broadway came in with $100,000." She told Broadway they could take the books off the market for $150K.

I'm floored. I say, "Are you f---ng kidding? Oh, my good God..."

I call Rajeev and leave two messages. Meanwhile, Claudia comes back with Jack's email. He says it's a great good fortune to sell three books into this marketplace.

Claudia says, "Doesn't he realize we're Religious Scientists?" (I.e., fortune has nothing to do with it.)

I tell Claudia to sit down. After all the talk of how fine $20,000 is, how fine Avon is, how I should be pleased to be published at all—Broadway came in with $100K.

Another call comes in. It's Rajeev. I tell him about the offer from Broadway. He says, "F—k me."

Then call comes in and it's Pocketbooks at $105K.

Called Keith and said, "Oh my God, there's a bidding war." I tell him I'm buying lunch Tuesday. He says, "It's on us, regardless. You're going to buy a house, right? I worry, you know."

I said, "Right." [*Ed.– No, she didn't.*]

He said that when he told Joel and Mike about the original offers, they were impressed at levels of $30,000 and $27,500: "Hey, that's *real* money."

Rajeev calls. I tell him about the counter-offer from Pocketbooks. I say, "I'm not even showered." He says, "I wouldn't, until 6 pm." I tell him: "This is why we didn't celebrate last night, because tonight is the night to celebrate."

Jenny keeps telling me, "I don't have a lot of time to spend on the phone" then hangs up.

Go, girl!

PS—Jenny said Ann Campbell at Broadway wants sex. I said, "Well you know I wrote for Playboy, don't you?" She said that she'd seen that in the bio, but didn't know if Ann knew it. I said I can do it, I just grind my teeth with embarrassment.

Let me get this straight. You want me to WHORE OUT my beloved characters for the prurient enjoyment of a bunch of PERVERTED READERS?

Okay, how many scenes?

3:19 pm

Just talked to Jenny. She said she had a splitting headache, is pounding Maalox and taking cigarette breaks every five minutes. She wants to have a long, *Aren't We Fabulous?* talk on Monday. She's made four deals today.

Broadway has offered $120,000, and everyone else has dropped out. I say (like an asshole), "What do you think we should do?"

Says she, "I think we should *take* it."

Ann Campbell (Senior Editor at Broadway) wants more spice. They want it to be a franchise, to brand it and release a book every six months. They'll put a real PR push behind it.

I said that's exactly what I wanted to hear.

I knew Jenny was the right person. I gave her all the credit. Told her other agents had said, "Lively, amusing, wonderful...not for me." She said, "They turned it down? We had four publishers bidding on this!"

She's worried about iUniverse. I said I didn't think it would be a problem. She said to let me know as soon as possible so she doesn't have to worry about that. She'll hold off on the announcement.

Just don't know what to say. It's all so fabulous.

Now this is the upshot (finally!): I said I wanted $50,000 per book, I got $40,000. But obviously they're going to pony up for the next one, probably on an outline. And I'll get money from foreign sales.[*]

I DID IT FOLKS, IN TWO AND A HALF YEARS!

---

[*] The first two books were sold to a German publisher for 10,000 Euros each, bringing the total close to my stated goal of $50,000 per book.

(With a teensy bit of help from God.)

When looked at like this—a good deal for three books in just two and a half years—it seems like a ridiculously short amount of time. But it felt like an eternity. I spent every day writing and editing, logging onto the Internet, praying for someone to give me a review, receiving very little encouragement other than that coming from my buddy in consciousness, Claudia.

Keeping a positive mental attitude is damn hard work that seems to stretch out forever in front of you. You can't know with absolute certainty when things are going to turn around, but you must hold onto the idea that you are *making* it happen. Writing down what you intend to happen is essential, as is visualizing it in meditation. You have to keep the faith that in the end you'll deliver your dreams in physical form, even though the gestation period can seem endless.

There was another fun synchronicity here. As it turned out, Broadway Books was an imprint of a much larger publisher. By June 2005 I would indeed be holding a book in my hand that was released by…wait for it…

Random House.

It had been an intensive, all-day auction that took place on Shakespeare's birthday. I saved a copy of the announcement that was eventually posted in Publishers Marketplace [*Ed.–This one is real, not a product of Jennifer's imagination*]:

4 May, 2004

> fiction Previously self-published author Jennifer Colt's
> THE BUTCHER OF BEVERLY HILLS, THE
> MANGLER OF MALIBU CANYON, and THE
> VAMPIRE OF VENICE BEACH, chick lit crime
> novels with "a fun, Janet Evanovich feel," to Ann
> Campbell at Broadway, in a good deal, by Jenny
> Bent at Trident Media Group (world English).

Compare this one with the one I made up only months before, featured in the previous chapter. How eerie is that?

It was a good thing I'd received encouragement *but not the top prize* from the PWA/St. Martin's contest. If I'd won, I would have received a ten thousand dollar publishing contract for a single book. As it was, I would be paid twelve times that amount for three books. It was also fortuitous that I'd been rejected by all those other agents because Jenny turned out to be the best agent I could possibly have.

The moral of the story is to make your desires known to God, but don't try to tell Him/Her/It how to do His/Her/Its job. Leave some room for an even bigger demonstration than the one you may have envisioned.

It was one (say it with me...)

BIG-ASS MIRACLE.

A small detail remained before my deal was finalized—the iUniverse issue. I tried to be at ease, asserting that my consciousness would smooth the way for me, but Jenny wasn't so sure: "I don't want Broadway backing out of the deal!"

I told her not to worry. Everything else had worked out and this would, too. Inwardly, though, I was sweating it. I continued to pray and was gratified a couple of days later to receive an email releasing me from the agreement—a "minor mercy" following the main miracle.[*]

I spoke to my new editor, Ann, who told me how happy she was to be publishing these books. She said everyone at Broadway was very enthusiastic about them. I'd be getting my contract soon, she promised.

The deal was done; the gift was made.

Tip: Guess what I'm going to say. Go ahead, use your expanded mind to guess what I'm going to say here.

I know, I know. I sound like a broken record, but…

---

[*]Your "BAM" will frequently be accompanied by the Minor Mercies, who are like cheerful little pilot fish that follow the Miracle Shark around, gobbling up snags in the unfolding of your prayer.

Imagine if I didn't have a journal with a contemporaneous *reportage* of what I'd wanted and prayed for, and all of the things that came about as a result.

How would I ever prove it to myself, let alone to you, Dear Reader?

Actually, I don't have to imagine what that would be like because I've tried telling people face to face about this stuff on multiple occasions. Know what happens? They look at me funny. *Real* funny.

Do this for me, please. Write it all down.

Then "Dig your ditches and wait for rain" becomes "Write your life and wait for it to play out just as you imagined it."

Professional intuitive Laura Day takes it even further, suggesting that you pen a "reality tale," a narrative account of what you'd like to see happen in your life—something like the following:

"I woke up Thursday morning and stumbled over to the computer to check my Lotto ticket online and *ohmygodinheavenIwonIwonIwon…!* I called Mom to tell her and she said, "Are you drunk?" and I said, "No, Ma! You're gonna have that Winnebago you've always dreamed about! The one with the flat-screen TV and the Mag wheels and the flames painted on the side!"

I've done this sort of thing many times. I've also written myself little scripts using screenwriting software, which I describe in more detail in Chapter 20.

This works. It really, really works.

End Tip

16

There is no "Anyway"

My little sister was so thrilled she was almost breathless when I called to tell her about my publishing deal. Her excitement waned when she heard me declare that I'd done it all with R.S.

"You did it with your *talent*," she chided me. "I don't think every successful writer out there has achieved what they have using R.S."

Both of my sisters correctly believe that I am lacking in self-esteem. This was my younger sister's way of urging me to take credit for my efforts and ability, and I appreciated what she was trying to do, but—

"I can't tell you how other people do it, I can only tell you how I did it. And I did it with prayer, visualization, and journaling. How many *other* talented writers are languishing out there without a publishing deal? And how often have you heard about a person starting out as a novelist, writing three books in quick succession, and landing a deal for all three in just two and a half years?"

She had no comeback when I put it that way.

I'll admit, I don't know what's "true" about the situation. I only know what I believe to be true.

That's all anyone can tell you about anything.

My belief is that if you trust in divine guidance, you will find your way. Trust that the right thing will happen at the right moment, even if it doesn't look that way from your present vantage point. Stop all of your fears in their tracks. Laugh in their faces. Then pray as if the thing you desire is already on its way to you.

I'd like to honor the skeptics at this point by saying I understand your objections. I know the flipside of everything I've asserted in here. You could argue that my synchronicities are sheer coincidence, and that I'm inferring connections where there are none. Also, that I remember the things that support my thesis, conveniently forgetting the ones that contradict it. You can and probably will argue that these things I prayed for and received were "going to happen anyway."

But guess what?

There is no "anyway."

Quantum physicists have proven that we do not live in a mechanistic universe in which things proceed in a logical, linear fashion like clockwork. We *change* reality in the process of observing it, interacting with it. *We are the clock and its works.* Our thoughts, actions, observations, and measurements are what nail down what we call reality out of all the quantum potentialities that exist.

154

In other words, we're making everything up.

It's possible to describe the process, impossible to really comprehend it. But you can still use these techniques, even if you don't understand why they work. How many people understand what happens when they flip a light switch, or turn on their computers? Doesn't stop them from using electric lights or the Internet, does it?

Does a circus chicken understand why food appears when it pecks a button? *Doubtful.* Does it grasp the intricacies of the mechanical feeder? *I'm guessing not.* That doesn't stop it from gulping down the mullet, does it?

No, because despite their reputation chickens are *not* stupid enough to turn down free food. We, on the other hand, will fight abundance all the way because we don't understand how it comes about.

If you're offended by the comparison of human intelligence to a chicken's, I would submit that vis-à-vis our understanding of the universe, it's too flattering an analogy. We're more like paramecia trying to stage a moon landing.

Listen, nobody has to believe this because I do. Nobody has to believe *anything.* However, if you don't like the way things are going in your life, please know this:

You have the power to make up something entirely different.

It requires a tough mental attitude, but if you try to believe that you're going to see a change in your life, eventually you will.[*] My skeptical friends might want to point out that I haven't achieved all of my goals. I don't have a perfect marriage. I'm not a bestseller. I'm not well off. Matter of fact, I'm scraping bottom *again*.

My answer is that there was a time when I would have considered myself very rich indeed to have spent ten years doing nothing but writing. I've seen my name on a screen and I've had three books in print with a major publisher. Maybe that's the extent of my miracle-making power, but there are lots of people out there trying to do as much. I'm pleased to have accomplished those goals, and I'll say it again:

I did it with Spiritual Mind Treatment.

In the early days, I read all the mysteries I could get my hands on. Once I saw an interview with an established author who was asked what advice he would give to new writers.

"I'd tell them to go into *any* business other than publishing," he snarked.

Here was an award-winning novelist with some thirty books listed in his bibliography, several of which had been made into movies, and he was cracking cynical about things the rest of us could only dream of.

Who was he to discourage anyone? How was it possible for him to know what's in someone else's future, who may have a completely different experience from his, and who

_____

[*] Or instantly, if you're Claudia.

certainly will if he or she understands that *we* create our life circumstances, not the other way around?

If you want to be a writer, don't listen to him. Don't even listen to me. Go where God is and hold up a sign that says HELP! See where it takes you.

 **Tip: There is no "Anyway"**

You are making up your life.

All of it.

Really.

End Tip

17

Delayed, but not Denied

After Jenny closed the publishing deal, I busied myself with injecting more romance into the stories per Ann's request while I waited for my contract to arrive.

And waited.

And *waited.*

Was I worried? Nah, I was too busy revising the first three manuscripts, plus writing a fourth. Every now and then, say, when my friends or my cousin or my in-laws or my sisters asked for the thousandth time, "Where's your contract? Why don't you call your agent? Is this deal real? Why won't you just *call*?" I'd get a wee bit anxious.

It wasn't that I was superstitious, but I was afraid that pushing too hard would cause the miracle to melt away. You know that there's a little devil who lives on your shoulder, right? Nasty little bugger. Mine's named Devlin.*

---

* If you're concerned about the number of voices I have in my head, please bear in mind that I'm a novelist. It's an occupational hazard.

Devlin sat there whispering in my ear, "Nothing works out for you, it always falls apart. If they were really going to publish you, *you'd have that contract by now.*"

I'd backhand him and he'd go tumbling to the floor, then I kept on working. I tried not to give him the satisfaction of showing it, but his words *had* stung. Would this turn out to be another failed venture? Would the excitement of auction day turn into despair?

Not yet, anyway.

My patience was rewarded five months later. The contract finally arrived and just like that—

BAM.[*]

My dream of being published became a reality.

Tip: Tell your version of Devlin to suck it.

Say to him: "Okay, smart guy, you think you can do better? Well, get on over here. Let's see you try.

Oh, wait. You say you *can't* come over here and try because you…*what*? Have no fingers to type with? No hands *with* fingers? No body to sit in the chair…?

---

[*] (B)ig-(A)ss (M)iracle

Oh my God, you're not real, are you? You're just a disembodied voice in my head, a tape running over and over telling how much I have to fear from sticking my neck out!

Why, you're no more substantial than...a *thought*.

Well, Devlin the Devil, you're a fired thought.

I'm hiring someone else to sit on my shoulder and whisper in my ear. Someone with a sunnier disposition, more pep in her step. Someone who'll give her all for the home team. And I believe I'll call her...

Angelika.

Yeah, Angelika the Angel.

Somehow I think she'll make a better muse."

End Tip

18

Fasten Your Seatbelts, It's Going to be a Bumpy Career

*W*hen I wasn't looking, feminism went out of style. Women began referring to themselves as girls, to be followed by the even more retro "ladies" and of course the formerly *verboten* B-word.

I know the terms are used ironically; I use them that way myself. But something uncomfortable was happening with regard to the position of women in society. Scholarly books and articles were being written about the backlash to the women's movement. Fashions became more frilly. Women were leaving career-track jobs to have babies and not returning to work.

I didn't think we were in danger of losing the right to vote or to own property again, but there was a strong whiff of boredom in the air. Young women seemed to think that feminism was so *yesterday*, taking for granted advances that had only come about in the years since they were glued to the tube watching *Scooby Doo*.

Don't get me wrong. I think it's good that we're no longer stomping around in shoulder pads smoking Tiparillos and pulling moves like Lorena Bobbit, but *sheesh.* Do we need all this thrashing back and forth? Talking about "enlightened sexism" and all that? Can't we women just consider ourselves people without whom *nobody* would be here in the first place, people who have equal, God-given rights with men, and without whose influence we would no doubt be embroiled in an endless state of war...? (Oh, wait. Scratch the last one.)

I was never a fan of *Sex and the City.* I didn't care to revisit my single years, which were hardly a swirl of fashion and cocktails and hunky boyfriends, but a singularly frustrating time. I suppose that's the whole point of the show—a romantic fantasy you could never achieve in real life—but I couldn't bring myself to watch it.

It's possible that I was the last person in the free world to read *Bridget Jones' Diary.* I thought it was screamingly funny, but still just considered it "comedy." Hard though this may be to believe, I didn't realize that a phenomenon called *Chick-Lit* was sweeping the nation.[*]

Imagine my surprise when I learned that I was a chick-lit author!

Oh well, it could have been worse. Chick-lit was quickly followed by *Mommy Lit* (which I didn't qualify for), and then by the oh-my-god-no *Hen Lit* (which I kind of did).

My new editor said that in addition to pumping up the romance, I had to describe the girls' clothing. It was *de rigeur* for

---

[*] Aquarians are famous for being either ahead of their times, or sadly lagging behind them. I manage to be a little of both.

authors of chick-lit books to dress their characters up like paper dolls.

"I haven't been out of the house in five years," I wailed. "I don't know what people are wearing. You have to help me with that!"

And help me she did, inserting brand names into the action, describing clothing I had no idea existed: Miss Sixties jeans, purple Pumas, a scoop-neck T-shirt.

The girls would sit down on the curb next to their Harley to mull over a murder, and Kerry would say: "Could *he* have been the one to kill her?" I asked, tugging on the sleeve of my baby T.

Jenny had won some important concessions in her long negotiations with Broadway. I knew I had the right to refuse changes, so when I saw Kerry crawling along the floor of a plastic surgeon's office wearing an A-line skirt, having traveled to the office by motorcycle only to be knocked unconscious by an unseen assailant and lie there sprawled in said A-line skirt, I drew the line.

The girls may be fashionable, but they ain't *stupid.* They're not going to be riding around on motorcycles chasing murderers in short skirts.

The book was neither fish nor fowl—neither a straight-ahead mystery nor a typical chick-lit offering. This caused some consternation in the marketing department, leading to a somewhat confused approach.

163

The first cover I saw was a cartoonish line drawing of the girls standing next to their motorcycle with their dogs at their feet. Terry was in a provocative pose, holding a gun in both hands. (They don't use guns in my books). Kerry was coquettishly looking out over the top of her designer sunglasses.

I loved the artwork, but wasn't sure what message it conveyed. It looked like an updated Hardy Boys. Who was going to pick up this book?

Turns out it was scratched because the drawing looked strange in color.

The next version I found (on the Internet) was hot pink and orange, with animated text, palm trees, and a silhouette of a crouching woman aiming a camera with a telephoto lens. I loved its retro 60's look, kind of like a James Bond novel. (I'll post these on my website.)

This latest cover adorned the business cards I took to my first mystery convention in 2005, called West Coast Crime. I met up in El Paso, Texas with my cyber friend, author Brian Wiprud. He and I had been corresponding since we were both at iUniverse, and now the two of us had deals with major publishers.

Brian was much more knowledgeable about the business than I was. He explained to me about ARCs (advanced reading copies), which he said I'd receive about six weeks before publication, recommending that I look up mystery stores online and send them review copies.

"Won't the publisher do that?" I asked.

He assured me that I'd better plan on supplementing the publisher's efforts with my own. They didn't knock themselves out for first-time authors.

Broadway actually did a lot to support me, which I only understood after the fact. I learned through a newsletter of the Mystery Writers Association that I'd seen my books on the front tables in Barnes and Noble and Borders bookstores because the publisher had paid for the "real estate."

Educating myself on the publishing business was the reason I'd gone to the convention in the first place. They invited me to speak on a panel moderated by (now) bestselling author Barry Eisler, with the topic: *Violence: How Much is Too Much?*

My books were comedic, no real rough stuff. I thought I must be there as a ringer. Before the session started I asked one of the attendees what constituted excessive violence, in her opinion.

"Beheadings," she said.

"Oh, I guess I do have a couple of those in *Mangler*...but it all happens off-screen!"

Though I was terrified to be speaking in public, I managed to vamp my way through the panel. I got some laughs describing a scene that was cut from the book, in which a pet pug is found chewing on the breast implant of a murder victim. The dog was left to starve when its mistress was stabbed, so it had done a little snacking while waiting to be rescued.

My sister agreed that I'd gotten a bit carried away. In particular, she had to skip a portion of the book describing a facelift, a procedure I'd seen on TV. Nevertheless, she became my biggest fan. She said the book was so attuned to her (our) sense of humor, it was like having her own private novelist.

I'd found my true voice at last.

One day a shipment arrived containing my ARCs. Trembling with excitement, I sliced the tape on the box and ripped it open.

What the what??

The James Bond vibe with the hot color palette had been replaced with a cartoon image of the twins standing outside the Beverly Hills Hotel in pastel shades. They were posed like fashion models holding a motorcycle helmet and a magnifying glass. A very girly look, if you didn't count the bloody knife lying on the ground.

Nobody had told me they were going with such a different look. It was cute but I'd become attached to the other cover. These were the ARCs that were sent to reviewers and stores. Would they know what to make of the book?

Imagine my surprise when the *actual* books showed up, and they looked like this:

I liked this one so well I forgave them for driving me crazy with all of the previous iterations. The graphics were eye-catching, and I especially loved the silhouettes up in the corner. The tagline was also very clever: "Two Pairs of Private Eyes are Better Than One."

Back was the hot color scheme with the somewhat edgy feel. It reminded me of Carl Hiaasen's books.

Around this time I received an email from the publicist, congratulating me on a great review from Publishers Weekly: "This is a fast-paced, gum-snapping, snarky chick-lit mystery with sparkle to spare." They were really happy about it at Broadway.

She suggested I go to bookstores when *Butcher* was released in order to sign copies. What she neglected to tell me was that it would be several days *after* publication that the books would show up on the shelves. I went around like an eager puppy with a sharpie in its mouth, offering to sign books that weren't there. In some cases, I was too embarrassed to go back.

Friends emailed me to say that *Butcher* had been spotted in various bookstores. I persuaded them to photograph themselves holding the book in far-flung locales like Toronto and London. Rajeev's brother was on his way to Japan at the time of the publication. He snapped photos of my sister-in-law with a group of her friends, holding the book on a Tokyo street like excited customers who'd stood in line all night to get a copy. (She'd taken it with her.)

This I called "Butchie's World Tour." The photos are up on my Facebook page for your enjoyment, as are the photos from my other whirlwind tours, which consisted of readings at the Barnes and Noble on Third Street in Santa Monica and at the Mystery Bookstore in Westwood.

I had discovered that most authors didn't actually read at these events, instead simply chatting with the audience about their books. Talking about my books made them sound like they were written by someone on crack. They're too wild and silly, they have to be read.

But reading aloud from them wouldn't work, either. I hit upon the idea of using hand puppets, sound effects, and other gags to support my interpretations. One time I obliged the audience to sing Barry Manilow karaoke during the reading for *The Hellraiser of the Hollywood Hills*. The events were a howl, even if they were attended by more friends than fans.

For some reason Broadway wasn't able to get many reviews. There was one in a new magazine called *Pages* that described my writing as "smart," and the book as a "true original." I subscribed to the magazine, but it lasted only two issues.

Entertainment Weekly was set to do a review at one point. I alerted everyone to the possibility, even telling them which issue to watch for. But when it was published, the review wasn't there.

A nearly identical experience happened with an NPR contributor later on. She called to say she was going to feature *Vampire of Venice Beach* in her "Summer Reads" segment, and wanted to make sure she had her facts straight. I told everyone I knew to listen to *All Things Considered*, but the review was ultimately cut. She apologized, explaining that her producer at NPR had made the decision. It stayed on the website, though.

One day the publicist called with some news that sent me into a major tizzy. She'd booked me on a local cable access show. Doing events in bookstores was nerve-racking enough, but going on TV was a horror in the making. What if I imploded? What if I started shaking so hard they had to cut the interview short and call 911?

The morning of the interview I told Rajeev that I *really, really* didn't want to do it.

Still, I'd done many things in my life I hadn't wanted to do, from piano recitals to business presentations, so I headed out to the interview. I wanted Broadway to see me as a trouper, and I knew that if I took a step in the direction of the studio, my body would somehow go through the motions and complete it, the way my fingers went through the motions writing screenplays or books.

Being too jumpy to trust myself on the freeway, I took Sepulveda Boulevard north to the Valley. As I got farther along, I began to notice that all of the traffic lights were out. There were no blinking yellows, no traffic cops on the scene. When I reached the studio, a man ran up to me and yelled, "Where did you come from?"

I didn't know what to say. "Texas? Venus?"

Then I noticed that people were milling around outside the studio, looking exasperated. The host, who was seated on a chair in the parking lot, introduced herself.

"The power's out in the neighborhood," she told me. "The studio's dark. Can we reschedule for tomorrow?"

The power outage was not a city-wide brown-out; only a small area including the studio had been affected.

Did I knock out the electricity with my amazing super mind powers in order to avoid the interview? I don't know, but I laughed all the way back down Sepulveda.

When I returned the next day, the power had been restored. Somehow I got through the interview, but I compensated for my nerves by acting goofy. That's something I do a lot.

It didn't help that the host was weirdly hostile to me during our pre-show chat on the stage. While they tested the lighting and angled the camera, she asked me about the screenwriting I'd done, wanting to know if I was a member of the Writer's Guild. I said no, but didn't have a chance to explain that Guild signatories are exempted on low-budget films before she blurted, "Doesn't that make you a *scab?*"

Guk!

They started rolling and she turned to the camera with a smile. "Today we have with us Jennifer Colt [THE SCAB], who's written a mystery called *The Butcher of Beverly Hills.*"

She turned back to me and opened with: "Your character Terry is a lesbian and a real potty mouth." Then she pursed her lips and cocked her head as if to say, "Comment?"

What was *up* with this dame? Why did she hate me? Did she suspect I'd mentally knocked out her power the day before?

I offered the explanation that as a lesbian, Terry is something of an outsider, which gives her the freedom to say or do anything she wants. She knows she'll always be rejected to some degree by polite society, so she might as well stick it to them. Terry was my favorite kind of character, an underdog whose outspokenness and in-your-face attitude I considered admirable.

The interview went from bad to worse. The host *really* hated it when I made jokes about the seventy-somethings who get their faces lifted in Beverly Hills. The lady herself was of a certain age, and it turned out that she, too, hailed from the world's most glamorous city.

I should have been comforted by the reaction of the production assistant, who ran up to me after the taping to say that it had been so funny she'd had to move to the back of the warehouse to keep her laughter from being picked up by the sound equipment. But I was only too happy to hop in my car and get out of the Valley.

The host's reaction to my work was typical of some people—those who complain that books like mine do nothing to "make them smarter." My response is that science has proven that laughter makes you both smarter *and* healthier. People who watch a funny movie before taking a test statistically score higher than their wound-up counterparts, and it's been shown to improve immune function, as well.

Not to mention, it can make life a whole lot easier to bear.

Tip: Be yourself at all costs.

People may not always appreciate you, but the simple fact is that *you* are the one who has to get up every morning and look at yourself in the mirror. *You* have to feed and clothe yourself, *you* have to do your job or raise your family, no one else.

Don't be afraid of judgment.

You'll *never* become happy trying to please other people. If you go about trying to prove your worthiness to them, you will only confirm their idea that you were unworthy in the first place, or why would you be trying so hard to convince them?

But if you go around being You, what can they do?

Shoot you?

Okay, they can shoot you. But what can they do legally? Not a whole lot.

Know thyself.

To thine own self be true.

Furthermore, love being You.

Think about this: You get to be You all day today! What could be more fun? *You* are a creative genius, inventing yourself from minute to minute, making up a whole human existence out of thin freaking air.

What a gas!

End Tip

19

Bye Bye Broadway

*M*y time as a Random House novelist was spent in self-promotion, as per the conventional wisdom. I embraced my inner chick (the outer one was teetering on menopause) and touted the heck out of those books. I went to mystery conventions; spoke on panels; visited stores to sign copies that sometimes weren't there; made friends on Myspace and then on Facebook; blogged; attended meetings of the local chapters of Sisters in Crime and the Mystery Writers of America; I gave out hats and bookmarks at the West Hollywood Book Fair and the LA Times Book Festival; I did my puppet shows and sent the books out for review.

Nevertheless, when the Spring of 2007 rolled around, it was clear they weren't going to be huge successes, despite the mock-ups on my wall showing them on the *New York Times* bestseller list. That year I was dumped by Broadway. To be more precise, they didn't exercise their option on my next book.

Jenny was still speaking to me, but Ann would soon leave the publisher to spend time with a daughter I didn't know she had birthed.

There were two more completed manuscripts in the series, *The Hellraiser of the Hollywood Hills* and *The Con Artist of Catalina Island*. They'd both been finished by late 2005 shortly after *Butcher* was released. I'd been so busy promoting myself in the interim that nothing else had been written.

When I contacted Jenny about the fourth book, she said she didn't see the point in running it past Broadway. My contract gave them the first option on the manuscript, and on the off-chance that someone else picked it up, I didn't want to be in breach. She went ahead sent it, receiving this response:

May 4, 2007

Dear Jenny,

Thank you so much for letting me have a look at Jennifer Colt's option material, THE HELLRAISER OF THE HOLLYWOOD HILLS (I do love the title), but I'm sorry to report that I'm going to pass. As you know, all of us here at Broadway are big fans of Jennifer and the irrepressible twins. I truly enjoyed working on these books and we had high hopes for the series; we put a considerable amount of marketing muscle into launching the books and breaking them out. But unfortunately, it proved to be a very tough road and they just didn't find a substantial audience. Given the very low sales, we cannot continue with the series at this time, but my sincere hope is that Jennifer will team up with a publisher that has the magic touch, and that these books will find the success they absolutely deserve.

Jenny went on to speculate that we'd suffered from a downturn in the sale of trade paperbacks, as well as a backlash against chick-lit.

Now, not only do I have to worry about a backlash against feminism, I have to worry about the backlash to the backlash against feminism?!

Though I never wanted to be marketed as chick-lit, the truth is, the brief popularity of that genre is what got me the deal in the first place.

It was all over. I was a failure at the most important thing in my life. Devastated, I lay down on The Magic Bed and hoped to die. What was the point of continuing? My life had no meaning...

Gotcha!

Sure, I was disappointed, but I was not about to lie down and die. I figured that just as on so many occasions before—being fired by Miramax, not winning the PWA/St. Martin's, being turned down by every agent in the world except the right one—this would prove to be a blessing in disguise. I didn't know how quite yet, but for some reason I couldn't fathom at the time, it would turn out to have been for the best.

Ltg 05-09-07

Just got a .pdf version of my official turndown from Broadway.

At another time, in another mindset, I would feel that everything was slipping away from me. Well, it's not. It is becoming what it needs to become by dint of thought.

Dear Reader, may I confess that at this point, even *I* am sick of my can-do attitude? I want to say: *Past Self, give it up already! Get a real estate license or some damn thing!*

Nevertheless, with the encouragement of a friend I decided to go the DIY route again. After a vacation trip to Maui, I was all fired up to make self-publishing magic once again.

It was six months until Christmas, plenty of time to ready *Catalina* for publication. The book takes place in Avalon at yuletide, so what could be better? The fact that it would be released out of order was problematic, but I solved that problem by calling it the sequel to the fourth book, which was the prequel to this one, which would be released next. Confused? It's easy: It goes one, two, three, five, four.

Being my own publisher turned out to be expensive and time-consuming. Instead of doing it POD (print on demand) as I had with iUniverse, I decided to give myself a promotion to hardcover. This meant that the interior had to be designed for offset printing, and the finished books would have to be warehoused with a distributor. Details that were usually taken care of by the publisher were my concern now: I had to obtain an ISBN (computer code), and LCCN (Library of Congress Control Number); I had to design the cover; update the website; get a re-sale license; establish an account with the distributor, Baker & Taylor; approve the design, and so on.

I printed paperback ARCs and sent them to bookstores and reviewers. For the dust jacket, I chose to go with expensive gold leaf, and wrangled with the printing agent until they gave me a perfect fire engine red for the background, in keeping with the Christmas theme.

Here's an excerpt from this period:

Ltg 08-28-07

This weekend, when I was in the throes of editing Catalina, Rajeev and I had one of our "life is good" sessions.

Only a couple of years ago the sessions went like this: Wow, you're working for [movie star filmmaker] and I'm being published by a major NY publisher!

Now, the sessions go like this–

Rajeev: I don't hate my new job and even though you're having to self-publish, our lives are still good, no?

It's true, they are.

The printing agent said that production of the hardcover book would require more time than the paperback ARCs. "How much longer?" I asked. "Around two extra weeks," he told me. I set the release date for mid-November based on his estimate.

The guy *may* have been new to publishing. When we were nearing the deadline he told me the extra time required would actually be six weeks, not two. I almost blew a gasket.

What would be the point of publishing a Christmas book in February?! Should I have it printed in China or something?

"No, they might be faster at printing," he told me, "but the books would have to be sent back to the US via ship line."

A slow boat from *China?*

I pleaded and threatened and must have done some first-rate cajoling, because the book was printed and ready to go on December 6th.

In one sense I lucked out. If the scheduling hadn't been so tight, I would have had to pay to warehouse the books until the distributor was ready to receive them. We thought they might even be shipped to our house, so we went out and cadged a wooden pallet from an alley, strapping it to the top of the car to get it home.

However, the delay in production meant that the books were loaded onto FedEx Freight trucks at the printer and taken directly to Baker & Taylor...*during the worst winter in recent history.*

So much for the luck. Snowstorms delayed deliveries all over the country. I kept logging onto the FedEx website to find that my books were stuck in one state after the other.

Merry Groundhog Day, everyone!

But finally they arrived at the distributor and were shipped out to bookstores, just in time for Christmas.

I'd done it.

The book was a thing of beauty. A bright red, gold, and green Christmas present for my readers. I couldn't have been more pleased, until I discovered a wee problem when I went to sign copies at the Mystery Bookstore. I frantically flipped the first pages back and forth, looking for the one with my name on it.

It wasn't there.

Now I know why they call it vanity publishing. My desire to see my name on a hardcover book, which I didn't even get to see because I'd left the stupid thing off, ended up leaving me thousands of dollars in the red.

Vanity, thy pen name is Jennifer.

Shortly thereafter, while setting up an account with Amazon Advantage to sell *Con Artist*, I came across a spanking new contest. It was called the Amazon Breakthrough Novel Award and they invited entries from all over the world to be judged by a panel of publishing industry experts. The top prize was a contract with Penguin Books.

Right about then, a contract with a traditional publisher who had their own printers and their own trucks was sounding pretty good. Sister had done it for herself and Sister was ready for someone else to do the heavy lifting.

And what do you know? Sister just happened to have another manuscript tucked away in a drawer.[*]

---

[*] Actually, it was on the hard drive.

Tip: Never let the bastards get you down.

Self-explanatory.

Next chapter.

End Tip

20

A New Petri Dish

*A*n author friend of mine just called with great news. Her book's sold out in the Netherlands and is going into a second printing. This is all the more impressive because she'd almost given up on the book entirely.

We became friends in 2005, fellow authors sharing our writing experiences and supporting each other through the publication process. One day in '06 she came over to my house, insisting that we watch a DVD called *The Secret*.

In case you are of Martian extraction and have not heard of it, I will explain *The Secret* to you in brief:

It's a documentary about the Law of Attraction, one of the universal laws discussed in *The Science of Mind*. It's no exaggeration to say the film took the world by storm, from the set of the Oprah Show to the peaks of Katmandu. Though the ideas are not new, the visuals and testimonials put them across in a way that's not possible with the printed word alone.

Of course, they left out the other universal laws Ernest Holmes talks about, the Law of Mental Equivalents and the Law of Cause and Effect, and not a lot is said about the active intelligence popularly known as God—but the book is always better than the movie, right?

One featured speaker, entrepreneurial coach John Assaraf, told the story of how he'd accidentally bought his dream house five years after placing a picture of that very house on his vision board—a wish list constructed like a collage. The process he described reminded me of the press release I'd mocked up for Future Self's future deal. When you put something in writing or depict it visually, imagining it as an accomplished fact, it's like designing the blueprint for your castle in the air. Afterward, the castle materializes on the Earth in solid form.

This concept goes all the way back to Plato's Idealism (and even further back than that). He believed that objects, animals, and human beings exist in some unseen realm before manifesting in the physical world. They continue to exist there in a perfect form, even as their physical manifestations undergo corruption and death here on earth.

I'd been telling this friend about my own experiences with prayer, but the movie really convinced her. She was determined to try this Law of Attraction stuff on her own.

I had a fresh new Petri Dish!

One of her novels had been turned down by the publisher a couple of years previously, causing a rift between my friend and her agent. She'd been forced to write a new book very quickly or lose the advance the publisher had paid, and the pressure had almost killed her. As soon as she could, she got rid of the agent who hadn't stood up for the original book.

One day she was talking to her mother about the need for money. Her mom suggested she take out the old manuscript and dust it off. I encouraged her to do it, too. She wasn't looking for a huge advance; she'd have been happy with ten thousand dollars. Agreeing that it was worth a try, she queried the publisher about it. They rejected it again, leaving her open to try other options.

Then along came a *new* agent who thought the book was great. This woman enthusiastically took it to market and landed a $40,000 deal for the original manuscript, plus another $40,000 for a sequel. In addition, they've sold several foreign territories. Apparently, she's very big with the Dutch. We'll see how she fares in China.

The thing is, she went from zero to $80,000+ at a time when the publishing industry was in a real slump and many people couldn't get a contract at all.

Was it beginner's luck? Or was it *The Secret*?

I report, you decide.

Tip: Don't "write" or speak what you don't want.

Even after this remarkable experience, my friend went back to being cynical about the publishing business.

While discussing her most recent project, she's said things like, "Well, after the lousy domestic sales of that book, I'll only get $25,000 for my next one, if it sells at all. And they'll want a sequel, too, which I don't feel like writing, and then I'll be stuck for another two years making no money..."

Would it be rude to say, "Bite your tongue, Missy!"

In outlining her worst expectations, she's actually causing them to come about. A talented writer, both on the page and in life, she's envisioned a miserable situation down to the tiniest detail. It's a very compelling reality tale.

She forgot to forget what she "knows"!

I have no doubt that if she continues to think this way, she will get exactly what she expects. On the other hand, is she *remembers to forget* what the "reality" of the situation is, she can write whatever outcome she wants.

I'll say it again:

Know what you want, state it in writing, meditate on it, and you're on your way to getting it.

The corollary to which is:

Know what you don't want, talk about it endlessly, and you're equally likely to get the thing you don't want, bringing it into reality through the operation of your vivid imagination.

Your choice. Utterly.

End Tip

21

Contest Whore

Yes, I know I'm always entering contests like some deranged, sweepstakes-addicted housewife.

What of it?

Having nothing to lose but my dignity [*Ed.– Please!*], I entered *Hellraiser* in the first Amazon Breakthrough Novel Awards. Five thousand manuscripts were submitted from twenty countries, making it a real long shot. The finalists would be critiqued by the panel of judges who were big names in the publishing business, but the actual winner would be chosen by *vox populi*. Whoever had the most votes from Amazon customers (or the author's friends and relatives) would take home the prize, a $25,000 publishing contract with Penguin Books.

As usual, I "treated" to win, but this time I added a new wrinkle: I went through the entire contest step by step in my meditations, hitting all of the pertinent dates. There were several rounds of eliminations over the course of a few months, culminating with the choice of ten finalists by Penguin.

Lying on The Magic Bed, I affirmed that on January 15th I'd make the first cut from 5,000 to 850. I imagined jumping for joy at the news, and then travelled forward in time to the next elimination on February 19th, when they would reduce the number to 100. I imagined myself receiving an email telling me I'd made that cut, and doing a little dance of joy afterward. On March 3rd I mentally enacted a scene in which I received a call from Amazon, telling me I was in the top ten. This time I jumped for joy *and* did a little dance. I really tried to feel the triumphs, the way that guy does in *The Secret*, pretending his easy chair is a Ferrari.

(Remember, no one can see inside your head while you're meditating. For all they know you're counting sheep.)

Here's how it looked in the L[istening To God] journal:

> January 15th, 2008: They announce the semi-finalists [in the Amazon Breakthrough Novel Awards]. I'm one of them.
>
> February 19th, 2008: I'm announced as one of the top 100 semi-finalists.
>
> March 3rd, 2008: I'm announced as one of the top ten finalists by Penguin.
>
> April 1st, 2008: I'm announced as one of the top three finalists in the ABNA contest. I'm going to NYC!
>
> April 5th, 2008: I arrive in NYC and have a blast for a couple of days!
>
> April 7th, 2008: I WIN THE CONTEST!!!

With my screenwriting software, I wrote scripts depicting the action on announcement days. They'd start out with me yawning as I sat down at my computer, logging onto my email account. In voiceover (a kind of thought bubble), I'd talk about how I was going to see the word *Congratulations*! in the subject line of an email:

Jennifer logs into her email account.

JENNIFER

(jumps out of her chair)

I did it! I knew I could do it, and I did!

I'm not going to reproduce the scripts in their entirety because, despite all evidence to the contrary, I do have some shame. They're really stupid, not to mention repetitive. Every single one features me sitting down at my computer with a cup of coffee, going all crazy when I get word from the contest.

True to the script, I sat down at the computer with a cup of coffee, and on the day of the first announcement:

Ltg 01-15-08

This is the day they announce me as one of the winners in the Amazon Breakthrough Novel contest. [*Ed.– It was the semi-finalists who were announced, not the winners. Jennifer is not awake yet.*]

Probably by the time Rajeev gets up, I'll have the word!

I logged onto my Hotmail account and this is what I saw:

Status of your ABNA entry

Jennifer,

Thank you for participating in the Amazon Breakthrough Novel Award. We received thousands of submissions and were impressed by the incredible talent and creativity seen in the entries. We are happy to inform you that you have been selected as a semi-finalist. Good luck!

ABNA Admin Team

Jiggle for joy! Squeak for joy! Can't dance and shout because Rajeev's still snoozing!

Did I cause this to happen by meditating on it? I really don't know. I can't go back and undo all the meditation. Nor can I unwrite my silly scripts. It's impossible therefore to know what the effect of *not* doing all of that would have been. This is one reason for believing in miracles, to hedge your bets. The French philosopher Blaise Pascal said (paraphrasing):

You might as well believe in God. There's no downside if you're wrong, but there's a big upside if you're right.

But what about the other contestants? Do you think none of them has ever seen The Secret or read Ernest Holmes? Were your prayers more fervent than theirs or something?

The answer is that I still don't know. All I can tell you is what I did, and what happened afterward. Sometimes you hit the mark, sometimes you don't. I don't pretend that every time I prayed for something it showed up exactly as I'd wanted. Obviously I'm not a *New York Times* bestseller, nor did Broadway pick up books four and five in my series for a nice advance. What you're looking for is an upward trajectory in your life. It doesn't mean you won't have setbacks, a few dips in the graph.

However, if you put enough mental energy into making miracles, some-*how* some-*thing's* going to come through for you. Your efforts in one area will bleed over into another. A woman I know who's into *A Course in Miracles* put it to me in this way.

There are only three possible answers to a prayer:

1) Yes.

2) Yes, but later.

3) No, I've got something even better in mind.

This is what I try to believe. The act of praying is the prayer itself. It's making your desires known to a receptive intelligence that is *designed* to manufacture them and then return those things to you in physical form, sooner or later.

Physicist David Bohm described reality in terms of an implicate order and an explicate order. He posited that the implicate or unseen order was the basis for the physical world—the dream factory that contains all possibilities within it. Those possibilities will then be brought into existence through interaction with consciousness. This is echoed in the Biblical saying: *from the unseen comes all that is created.*

It's very similar to the Platonic idea—a world that precedes the physical one, containing the products of imagination to be mirrored on the physical plane. What you appear to be doing when you envision a certain outcome is priming the creative force of the universe, this invisible, plastic stuff that can and will take any shape you desire down here on the Earth.

I know I'm repeating myself. That's deliberate. If you've never experienced the phenomenon of manifesting with thought, or if you've never believed in the creative power of the unconscious mind, perhaps it will help you overcome your skepticism to know that it's been talked about and talked about and talked about since the dawn of recorded history. Sure, there are people who disbelieve it, and many of them have letters behind their names and other impressive credentials.

But there have been many who *have* believed it, also brilliant, credentialed and accomplished: David Bohm, Plato, Ralph Waldo Emerson, R. L. Stevenson, William James, Sir James Jeans—I could go on.

It amounts to a choice. Really. No one has all the answers on either side of the divide. The question is, how do you want to live? As if all things are possible? Or as if you are hemmed in by a reality that will defeat you at every turn?

If you decide on the former, just know that you are in good company. You're hanging with Nobel laureates and scientists and philosophers and Harvard professors and writers and artists who have a lot more fun than the naysayers!

Now back to the contest. The semifinalists were granted reviews from *Publishers Weekly*, the most prestigious of literary magazines. (I forgot to thank PW in the acknowledgments for *Hellraiser*. Thank you, PW.)

Here's mine:

The Hellraiser of the Hollywood Hills: A McAfee Twins Mystery; Manuscript review by Publishers Weekly, an independent organization

Twin private investigators Kerry and Terry McAfee are used to working the sleazy side of Hollywood, but they get more than they bargained for when they save celebrity "It" girl Bethany from aggressive paparazzi and end up wanted for kidnapping.

The charges are dropped, thanks to their lawyer and friend Eli Weintraub and a convenient reality television show taping, and the whole thing may have been a publicity stunt for Bethany's up-coming tour, but something's not adding up. Bethany's manager hires the twins as the star's latest pair of bodyguards, only to have Bethany disappear in a stolen car. With the star on the loose and in disguise, the twins have their work cut out for them. Then people start turning up dead.

Fans of Janet Evanovich's "Stephanie Plum" series would be entirely at home with level-headed Kerry, wannabe-stuntwoman Terry, and their assortment of odd-ball friends and acquaintances, from a trio of helpful prostitutes to dog-sitter/actor/duck hatcher Lance Manley. Lively characters and plenty of action and humor make this mystery more than worthy of its wacky La-La Land setting.

It was a very positive review, but there were still many competitors, and plenty of them had good notices, too. Not everyone was a wannabe, either. I noticed several published authors among the contestants, confirming their identities by clicking through to their Amazon book pages. One guy had received blurbs from Stephen King. They'd produced movies from his books.

The only explanation I can offer is that the book business was in transition, and many writers had found themselves in the same position I had—kicked to the curb.

Next came another elimination round, when the contestants were whittled down from 836 to 100:

Ltg 02-19-08

Made it.

Made it into the top 100 in the ABNA contest.

I'm doing my compulsive analysis of who got in, and what's interesting is that many of the entries with an "A" rating (by my reckoning) from PW did not get in. Some B's, a couple of C's, a lot of A's—but not everyone had a lot of customer reviews.

So I've made two cuts, one from 5,000 to 836, and the next one from 836 to 100.

Around this time Rajeev and I went out for our usual Saturday Mexican lunch. Choosing my words carefully, I told him I thought I would finish in the top ten. His answer was guarded: "Yes, I think it's the best book so far. It has a good opening and—"

"No, no, no. I'm not saying it's *worthy* of being in the top ten. I'm saying that I feel I *will* be. I'm talking about intuition."

He didn't exactly pooh-pooh what I said, but we got off the subject pretty quickly.

The morning of February 25th I arose early and, yes, went to my computer with a cup of coffee. It was the day after the Academy Awards. When the phone rang, showing a 206 area code on the caller ID, I was confused. *Where's 206?* my thought bubble said. [*Ed.– You really don't want to talk to Jennifer first thing in the a.m.*]

I picked up the phone. It was Amazon calling.

Ltg 02-25-08 AMAZON TOP 10!!!

Just had the call from Amazon. Can I get a *This stuff really, really works?*

I can't believe it. I can, but I can't.

I thought they'd be calling people tomorrow at the earliest!

They called me at 8:11 [a.m.]. I look at the Caller ID and it's a 206 number, with someone named Aaron on the phone. I'm frowning at the handset wondering *who the hell*? Some sort of telemarketer? He asked for Jennifer Colt. I said, "This is she."

He said he was Aaron from Amazon, and my heart slowed down and my head suddenly went stupid, and he told me I was in the Top Ten of the ABNA contest!

The next order of business was to get the most votes à la *American Idol*. I sent an email to everyone I could think of, begging them to post a review the excerpt. Amazon began revving up the publicity for the contest, landing me an interview with my hometown paper.

Ltg 03-18-08

I have an interview with the Santa Monica Mirror today, which will be my practice for the L.A. Times! (Javier told me he was working on it.) Got to get my head around that.

Three of the panel experts weren't exactly keen on my book, but the fourth one had very nice things to say about it. She was Elizabeth Gilbert, the author of *Eat, Pray, Love.* (Oh, what does she know about writing? She's only sold *a hundred million books*.) Allow me to reproduce her words from the tattoo on my body:

"You can't teach someone to write like this; you are either born able to generate such wit or you'll never be able to learn it."

Bless you, Ms. Gilbert. I really enjoyed your book, too. I read it in Italy, then left it on the train from Florence to Rome for some lucky traveler to enjoy.

Still, when the final tally came in…

New Orleans Bartender Wins Amazon Breakthrough Award

By Lynn Andriani -- Publishers Weekly, 4/7/2008 7:55:00 AM

The winner of the first Amazon Breakthrough Novel Award was announced today: Bill Loehfelm, author of *Fresh Kills*, a noir mystery about lower-middle-class life in Staten Island, home to the famous garbage dump Fresh Kills. Representatives from Penguin and Amazon made the announcement at a breakfast at the Gramercy Park Hotel in New York City this morning.

I finished in fourth place. Bill Loehfelm appeared to be a cool guy with a great book. Although none of us got terrific reviews from the expert panel, he seemed to do the best. It was his contest to win, his turn to get a publishing deal.

I canceled a lunch date I'd made with a friend in New York, then notified all of my supporters about Bill's win. My friend Daphne McAfee in Toronto was crestfallen. She had planned to fly in for the occasion so we could Laverne and Shirley it all over Manhattan. She had a special stake in the success of the books because I'd named the twins after her.

Although I didn't get the $25K there *were* consolation prizes. Hewlett Packard sent me a fabulous computer from their entertainment series, a Pavilion PDX with all the trimmings. (One writer friend joked that it was better than many publishers' advances.) I received an all-in-one color printer, scanner, and copier. The HP man said that if I wrote a bestseller on the computer to let everyone know. Sorry, but it's too beautiful to be used for word processing. We've got it plugged into the DVR so we can download shows from Netflix and Hulu.com.

All in all, it was an interesting exercise in consciousness. I didn't make it to New York, but I had a real fun ride. One of the other prizes was a Total Freedom publishing package from Amazon. They'd just acquired the self-publishing company BookSurge, which they planned on folding into their existing digital publishing venture, CreateSpace.

There was still a very good chance that someone else would pick me up, so I didn't rush to take advantage of the self-publishing prize. The Penguin editors had raved about *Hellraiser* in a video on the contest web page. I had self-published *Catalina* and I'd placed in their contest. I'd worked my butt off for years, building my reading audience. I had a decent number of fans, and I'd received consistently good reviews. Hadn't I shown myself worthy?

I mean, what does a girl have to do to get published in this town...?

Tip: Show up over and over again, no matter how many times you "fail."

I love this saying, although I don't know who to attribute it to:

How many times would you watch a toddler fall while trying to take his first steps before urging him to give up on the whole undertaking?

Of course the answer is that you would *never* do such a thing. Walking is a necessary skill and a joy, a hallmark of being human, as is growth in every area of your life. And you do *not* grow by shrinking back from challenges or by becoming complacent in your present circumstances.

Go, try, do, be, want, miss, learn, fail, succeed, walk, run, *fall down*, get back up…

It's all part of the human experience.

No reasonable person will fault you for not giving up. They might want to pity you, but go ahead and let 'em. In the words of Terry Cole-Whittaker:

"What you think of me is none of my business."

Just keep growing, and let the rest take care of itself.

End Tip

22

A Girl Publishes with Createspace

I can't lie to you, I was pretty tired of it all by this time, what with the begging and hawking and self-promotion, and the money flying out the window the whole time. I didn't have much heart for publishing anymore.

But I kept getting emails from fans saying they were anxious to read the new McAfee Twins book, and after almost a year, during which I half-heartedly pursued other avenues of publishing, I decided to take the plunge once more into Print-On-Demand.

This time the process was painless, and the results were stellar. Things had come a long way from 2002, or even from 2007. CreateSpace took care of those niggling details like the computer numbers. They designed the interior to match the previous books, but gave the cover a new look that I *loved* —a total departure from the bright ones done by Random House.

It's gorgeous, featuring a thirties-era movie star looking skyward, the lashes of her enormous eyes reaching almost to her brows. In the background is a blur of headlights, a stylized depiction of Hollywood Boulevard. The model is framed in strips of 35mm film that are scratched and fading, like something from the glory days of cinema. My favorite part is the iconic Hollywood sign in the title.

It might have looked more like a James Ellroy novel than was warranted, but I didn't care. There was everything to be gained from giving the series a new identity. I felt sure that *this* book would be picked up by readers. Best of all, Amazon would handle the distribution to bookstores and libraries. There'd be no inventory, no trucks—it was digital all the way. I've made it available on Kindle, too, where it's currently doing pretty well.

Which brings us around to today. What's going on in my life right now?

We're in the midst of a world economic downturn, or perhaps at the tail end of it. Work has been scarce. Money tight.

And yet, in spite of the feelings of despair that want to well up in me, I know that being stuck is just part of the process, a *Go Straight to Jail* stop on the Monopoly board. There are untold riches around the corner on Park Avenue. I'll see them when I believe them.

I'm not responsible for the economic situation, but I am responsible for my personal experience of it. Painful as it is, my situation has been designed by me, for me, in order to get it through my thick skull once and for all what my true nature is:

I'm the spirit inhabiting this body I call me. I'm my own art project and my own science experiment. I'm my own avatar, and I'm using me to play the game of life.

And, as we all know—in the game of life, sometimes you win, sometimes you...

Write an
Epilogue

*R*emember the old *Lifetime* movies? I'm a huge fan. The story usually revolves around a solid and capable woman, whose life begins to unravel in a stunning cascade of bad luck.

Her name is Sandra. She's a hardworking, compassionate, and pretty darn good-looking woman for her age—a pediatrician with a four-bedroom house in the suburbs, two beautiful children, and a handsome, doting husband. Yes, everything is just as it should be in Dr. Sandra's world until—

One day she comes home to find that her entire life has been a lie.

It turns out that Sandra's husband has spent all their retirement on male hookers; her son's a meth dealer at the local grade school; her daughter's been purveying nude pictures of herself online. To top it off, the head of surgery at Sandra's hospital turns out to be the ringleader of an international crime syndicate that's been diluting antibiotics destined for third world children suffering from meningitis.

Oh my God, what a pickle! What to do?

What would *you* do?

I'll tell you what Sandra does:

She copes.

(They always friggin' *cope*, these Lifetime gals!)

Sandra pulls herself up by the ankle straps, reminding herself that she's a *strong, independent woman* and—usually with the support of a girlfriend who has her own coffee mug in Sandra's kitchen, her own seat at Sandra's breakfast counter, and who never seems to have anything pressing on her *own* time— puts everything back together by the end of the show.

Dr. Sandra divorces the husband, whose tearful apologies fall on deaf ears (*Fool me once, Brandon!*); checks the son into a rehab facility; sends a bounty hunter to bust the daughter out of the prostitution ring in the Emirates that was supposed to be a modeling agency; informs on the insurance fraudster to the District Attorney. And *then—*

She turns around to discover that the cute guy next door, who works with his hands and is a world-class cook, has just been widowed and has always carried a torch for...*Sandra.*

PULL BACK on a free-standing bathtub at the water's edge, the sky a fiery red. And as Sandra and The Hunky Neighbor share a passionate, backlit kiss, we

FADE TO BLACK.

THE END.

If there's ever a nuclear strike on my town, I want Sandra in charge of the emergency response. She'd have everybody outfitted in *Hazmat* suits and evacuated to shelters before whipping up a batch of oatmeal cookies for the National Guard and putting the finishing touches on her acceptance speech for Woman of the Year.

Look, I'm no Ninja Soccer Mom, and let's face it— things are not quite as bad for me as they were for Dr. Sandra. They're not even as bad as they were, say, thirteen years ago when my whole world came crashing down around my ears. Still, the situation feels rather tenuous.

But you won't see me taking decisive action, Sandra-style. For one thing, I hardly ever have occasion to wear ankle straps. For another, I prefer less *exhausting* solutions to my problems now. I've done all the struggling I want to do in this life and world crisis or no, I'm demanding a solution that I haven't foreseen and that doesn't involve getting my hands dirty. Instead of beating my brains out, I'm going to get a miracle.

What makes me so sure?

With these words I'm sending out an S.O.S. Based on past experience I expect it to bring me results, even if I can't say exactly what they'll look like. While Sandra's plucky attitude— or "pluckitude"—makes for fine cable TV fare, it may not always be the best way to deal with problems in real life.

Why not?

Because real life is *strange*, as I hope to have demonstrated in these pages. It doesn't follow the rules of the Lifetime movies, doesn't fit together neatly as we were told it should, and it certainly doesn't comport with what they taught us in Sunday school. Merely being "good" will not assure you of continuing happiness. We do not live in a meritocracy, as unfair as that sounds. Instead—

It is done unto you as you believe.

My financial picture looks grim, but here's the real miracle I experienced while writing this book:

In the process of reviewing my life, I've reminded myself of what I've accomplished with prayer in the past and I've found the determination to do it again. If that makes me sound like Dorothy Gale broadcasting live from Emerald City— well, I guess that's just who I am.

I've meditated and prayed my way out of problems before; I'll do it again.

Don't think I can?

Read the sequel and find out.

May God bless you and bring you

BIG-ASS MIRACLES,

Jennifer Colt

PS – And minor mercies, too.

Religious Science credo, adapted from Ernest Holmes's "What I Believe"

- We believe in God, the Living Spirit Almighty; one, indestructible, absolute and self-existent Cause. This One manifests itself in and through all creation, but is not absorbed by its creation. The manifest universe is the body of God; it is the logical and necessary outcome of the infinite self-knowingness of God.

- We believe in the incarnation of the Spirit in all, and that we are all incarnations of the One Spirit.

- We believe in the eternality, the immortality, and the continuity of the individual soul, forever and ever expanding.

- We believe that the Kingdom of Heaven is within us and that we experience this Kingdom to the degree that we become conscious of it.

- We believe the ultimate goal of life to be a complete emancipation from all discord of every nature, and that this goal is sure to be attained by all.

- We believe in the unity of all life, and that the highest God and the innermost God is one God.

- We believe that God is personal to all who feel this indwelling Presence.

- We believe in the direct revelation of Truth through our intuitive and spiritual nature, and that anyone may become a revealer of Truth who lives in close contact with the Indwelling God.

- We believe that the Universal Spirit which is God, operates through a Universal Mind, which is the Law of God; and that we are surrounded by this Creative Mind which receives the direct impress of our thought and acts upon it.

- We believe in the healing of the sick through the power of this Mind.

- We believe in the control of conditions through the power of this Mind.

- We believe in the eternal Goodness, the eternal Loving-kindness and the eternal Givingness of Life to all.

- We believe in our own soul, our own spirit, and our own destiny; for we understand that OUR LIFE is God.

—*Wikipedia.*

Recommended Books

- Adams, Scott – *The Dilbert Future: Thriving on Stupidity in the 21ˢᵗ Century*

- RH Jarrett – *It Works! (The Little Red Book)*

- Barker, Raymond C. – *The Power of Decision*

- Bartlett, Dr. Richard – *The Physics of Miracles*

- Bristol, Claude – *The Magic of Believing*

- Byrne, Rhonda – *The Secret*

- Chopra, Dr. Deepak – *The Spontaneous Fulfillment of Desire: Harnessing the Infinite Power of Coincidence*

- Crichton, Michael – *Travels*

- Day, Laura – *Practical Intuition*

- Hicks, Esther and Jerry – *Ask and It Is Given: Learning to Manifest Your Desires*

- Holmes, Ernest – *The Science of Mind*

- Lipton, Dr. Bruce – *The Biology of Belief*

- McTaggart, Lynne – *The Field: The Quest for the Secret Force of the Universe; The Intention Experiment*

- Radin, Dr. Dean – *The Conscious Universe; Entangled Minds*

- Scheinfeld, Robert – *Busting Loose from the Money Game*

- Schwartz, Dr. Gary – *The Truth About Medium; The Sacred Promise*

- Sheldrake, Dr. Rupert – *The Presence of the Past; The Sense of Being Stared At; Seven Experiments That Could Change the World; Dogs That Know When Their Owners are Coming Home*

- Shinn, Florence Scovel – *The Power of the Spoken Word; Your Word is Your Wand* (Public Domain; available for free on the Internet)

- Talbot, Michael – *The Holographic Universe*

- Targ, Russell – *Miracles of Mind*

- Walker, Dr. David – *You Are Enough: Always Have Been, Always Will Be*

- Wolf, Fred – *Taking the Quantum Leap*

- Zukav, Gary – *Dancing Wu Li Masters: An Overview of the New Physics*

*Be sure to check out the **BIG-ASS MIRACLE** Café online. Miracles on the menu!*

You can also find Jennifer on Amazon, Twitter, Blogger, and wherever fine authors are sold. http://www.jennifercolt.com.

Made in the USA
Las Vegas, NV
02 March 2022

44866519R00128